FUTURE SUCCESS

A BALANCED APPROACH
TO MEASURING AND
IMPROVING SUCCESS IN
YOUR ORGANISATION

FUTURE SUCCESS

A BALANCED APPROACH
TO MEASURING AND
IMPROVING SUCCESS IN
YOUR ORGANISATION

CHARLES BIRCH

Prentice
Hall

Pearson Education Australia
Unit 4, Level 2
14 Aquatic Drive
Frenchs Forest NSW 2086

Commissioning Editor: Nella Soeterboek
Senior Project Editor: Elizabeth Thomas
Cover and text design by Ramsay Macfarlane, Surry Hills, NSW
Typeset by The Type Group, Wollongong, NSW

Printed in Australia by Ligare Pty Ltd, NSW

1 2 3 4 5 03 02 01 00 99

ISBN 1740 09111 6

National Library of Australia
Cataloguing-in-Publication data

Birch, Charles
Future success: a balanced approach to measuring and
improving success in your organisation.

Bibliography.   ♭ 17.95
Includes index.
ISBN 1 74009 111 6.

1. Success in business.   2. Organizational effectiveness.
3. Business — Management.   4. Performance — Evaluation. I.
Title.

658

ISBN 1740 09111 6

FOREWORD

Performance measurement is the critical ingredient in successful organisations. For many years, commentators have been advocating a revolution in management accounting so that performance measures present a balanced view of an organisation. But still it is clear that very few organisations have implemented the essence of a balanced performance measurement system to become world-class organisations.

Charles Birch has written about the balanced scorecard in a way that challenges CEOs, managers and accountants to reconsider the role of performance measurement in providing the opportunity for organisations to become successful. This book is his call to action. It is about placing the last piece in the jigsaw puzzle, the piece that completes the picture.

Charles begins this controversial book by examining the traditional 'piecemeal' role that performance measurement has played in most organisations, and then explains the need for an integrated business measurement system. He presents each of us with eight reasons why our organisations need an integrated performance measurement system. Next he outlines and sets forth in an informative and easy-to-understand way the four dimensions of the balanced scorecard. Part 4 of the book summarises the major tools managers can use to design their own balanced scorecards so that their organisations can become leaders in the performance measurement arena. I found it useful that he included case studies of how differently sized organisations in both the private and public sectors can push forward with the design of their own scorecards. He concludes with a strategy for implementation of the balanced scorecard.

At the end of *Future Success*, the author presents a comprehensive list of sample performance measures to get you thinking about the many varied performance levers that organisations can use to measure what is important to help them in their quest for wealth creation.

If your organisation is not designing and implementing its own balanced scorecard yet—whether you are in the public or private sector, a national or mulitnational, CEO or manager—you need to read this book. At Ericsson Australia we have been adapting the principles of the balanced scorecard for several years. And, as in your organisations, it has taken time to adopt the new methods that will ensure that Ericsson Australia meets its full potential.

I strongly urge you to read this book, absorb the concepts and ideas advanced by Charles, and to make your own decisions and judgments on the merits of the balanced scorecard.

I commend this to you.

Graham Truran
Director—Commercial and Business Services
Ericsson Australia

CONTENTS

PREFACE

How often do you ask yourself 'How can I measure performance?' Once a week? Once a month? Never? Measuring performance is often not easy. In the performance measurement arena, you do not always get the results that you expect or want.

There is a solution. Two key words can put your organisation on the path to success: disciplined approach. The balanced scorecard system is a disciplined approach to performance measurement and management. Too often performance measurement programs fail because they are short sighted, ill conceived and unfocused. These handicaps can be traced to one source: the lack of a viable approach to performance measurement from the start.

This book has three primary objectives:

1. to provide a detailed examination of the conceptual grounding of the balanced scorecard performance measurement framework;

2. to consider the balanced scorecard design and implementation process and explore their implications; and

3. to examine how the balanced scorecard approach applies to a wide variety of management situations and strategic change issues across all types of organisations.

The people I have kept in mind as this book's readers include the busy executive or manager, business entrepreneur, service providers (e.g. lawyers, accountants and medical practitioners) and employees who action tasks on the basis of sound conceptual footing. All these individuals are held accountable for making timely judgements and must balance alternate pathways against practical constraints to find the innovative solution.

It is useful to think of *Future Success* as a three part problem. First, there is the need to explain the reasons for a new approach to performance measurement. Then there is the challenge of designing a tailored system to achieve competitive advantage in the marketplace. Finally, there is the challenge of integrating design with implementation as the system unfolds in the competitive environment.

Need, design, implementation and integration must all come together for an organisation to realise its full strategic potential. Innovation, unfortunately, cannot be reduced to checklists or specified procedures.

Measurement is the backbone which inextricably links strategy and its tactical execution. At one level, measurement ensures that the day-to-day operation of an organisation is aligned with strategy. At a second level, it drives organisational learning and growth, ensuring that strategy design can adapt to a dynamic, competitive environment.

Accordingly, it is my hope that through the insights, principles and examples used in this book, readers can acquire the building blocks to implement a similar system in their own organisations.

I have used the masculine gender throughout this book where it has not been possible to use neutral plural pronouns. This is because filling a text with he/she or him/her interferes with logical thought processes. Wherever the masculine gender is used, the female gender applies equally.

Charles Birch

Mallesons Stephen Jaques

Melbourne

April 2000

ACKNOWLEDGEMENTS

In the writing of this book, I have relied heavily on the experiences of many organisations, managers, small business operators and recognised industry scholars. They rate too numerous to mention. I am indebted to Donald Farrands. Don made the suggestion to me that I should write this book.

I am grateful to Robert Kaplan and David Norton whose article on the balanced scorecard in *Harvard Business Review* in 1992 was the inspiration for me to write a book on the balanced scorecard.

Needless to say, this book has also required enormous editorial assistance. Alex Trifonidis has excelled in setting out the content in a way that I never could. Zac Karlaftis played an integral role in structuring the chapters so that the concepts and ideas are presented in a logical and easy-to-follow manner. Felicity Pantelidis has checked that the technical and theoretical concepts from which I have drawn practical solutions are properly used. Trieu Owen and Joanne Melville did a tremendous job editing this book from first draft through several iterations, and Liz Thomas managed the production of the book. That they did this on an already hectic work schedule and remained cheerful and enthusiastic throughout is a remarkable feat. Thank you.

There is another kind of support that was crucial to the successful completion of this book. It was written during evenings, weekends and holidays. I would like to thank my parents, brother and sister, and my fiancée, Carmel Ferraro.

TABLES

PART

1

BUSINESS MEASUREMENT IS PIECEMEAL

Performance measurement explored

What is a performance measure?

Why do you need to measure?

What is the basis of a performance measurement system?

Why change the way we measure?

Why is change so difficult?

Wisdom is always an overmatch for strength. Phaedrus

For organisations to gain a competitive advantage, new management approaches and performance measurement systems are required. Companies can no longer be run as a collection of functional 'silos' whose primary goal is to achieve a local optimum, often at the expense of other functional areas.[1]

If your organisation is like most, the bottom line is the only line that matters. It is curious that in a time when we are living through the nuclear, computer and information ages, working hard to manage total quality, pledging ourselves to clients and learning to surf the internet, corporate performance is still measured in ways that Caesar would find reassuringly familiar.

Nevertheless, change is in the air. The impetus for this change is the dawning realisation that traditional financial measures simply cannot provide the information needed to manage complex organisations for competitive advantage.

You know that an organisation's measurement system has a huge but often understated impact on the behaviour of its managers and staff. What you measure is what you get. Traditional financial measures such as cash flow, return on investment, residual income and earnings per share do not always deliver that vital piece of information. How can they? For instance, there are so many variations of 'earnings per share'. For example, earnings before interest and tax, after-tax earnings, earnings before abnormals, earnings after extraordinary items, yearly-average share price, share price calculated by factoring out the impact of dividends.[2] When the daily papers quote, in relation to the share price of Australian companies, the earnings per share, who can say which variation the newspaper is using?

This chapter considers the nature of performance measures, the commercial reasons as to why organisations need to measure performance and key components of successful performance measurement systems.

WHAT IS A PERFORMANCE MEASURE?

Performance measures quantitatively tell you something important about your products and services, and the processes that produce them. They are a tool to help you understand, manage and improve what your organisation does. Performance measures let you know:

▶ how well you are doing;

- if you are meeting your goals;
- if your clients are satisfied;
- if your processes are in statistical control; and
- if and where improvements are necessary.

Performance measures provide you with the information necessary to make intelligent decisions about what you do.

A performance measure is composed of a *number* and a *unit of measure*. The number gives us a magnitude (how much) and the unit gives the number a meaning (what). Performance measures are *always* tied to a goal or an objective. Performance measures can be represented by single-dimensional units such as hours, meters, nanoseconds, dollars, number of reports, number of errors, number of employees and length of time to design. They can show the variation in a process or deviation from design specifications. Single dimensional units of measure usually represent very basic and fundamental measures of some process or product.

More often, multi-dimensional units of measure are used. These are performance measures expressed as ratios of two or more fundamental units. These may be units such as kilometres per litre (a performance measure of fuel economy), number of defects per thousand hours worked (a performance measure of an organisation's quality program) or number of on-time vendor deliveries per total number of vendor deliveries. Performance measures expressed this way almost always convey more information than the single-dimensional or single-unit performance measures. Ideally, performance measures should be expressed in units of measure that are the most meaningful to those who must use or make decisions based on those measures.

Most performance measures can be grouped into one of the following six general categories. However, certain organisations may develop their own categories, as appropriate, depending on the organisation's mission statement.

Effectiveness • A process characteristic indicating the degree to which the process output conforms to requirements. (Are you doing the right things?)

Efficiency • A process characteristic indicating the degree to which the process produces the required output at minimum resource cost. (Are you doing things correctly?)

Quality • The degree to which a product or service meets client requirements and expectations.

Timeliness • Measures whether a unit of work was done correctly and on time. Criteria must be established to define what constitutes timeliness for a given unit of work. The criterion is usually based on client requirements.

Productivity • The value added by the process, divided by the value of the labour and capital consumed.

Safety • Measures the overall health of the organisation and the working environment of its employees.

An ideal unit of measure possesses a number of attributes. It should:

▶ reflect the client's needs as well as your own.

▶ provide an agreed upon basis for decision making.

▶ be understandable.

▶ be capable of broad application.

▶ be capable of uniform interpretation.

▶ be compatible with existing sensors (i.e. a way to measure it exists).

▶ be capable of precisely interpreting the results.

▶ be economical to apply.

Performance information must support the mission statement from the highest organisational level downward to the performance level. Therefore, the measurements that are used must reflect the assigned work at that level.

WHY DO YOU NEED TO MEASURE?

Listed below are seven important benefits that result from the implementation of effective measurements.

Client intimacy • Measurements identify whether you are meeting client requirements. How do you know that you are providing the services and products that your clients require?

Establishment of knowledge limits • Measurements help you understand your processes, and confirm what you know and reveal what you do not know. Do you know where the problems are?

Improvement in decision making • Measurements ensure decisions are based on fact, not on emotion. Are your decisions based upon well-documented facts and figures, or on intuition and gut feelings?

Improvement in initiatives • Measurements show where improvements need to be made. Where can you do better? How can you improve?

Monitoring of business performance • Measurements show if improvements have actually happened. Do you have a clear picture?

Uncovering of problems • Measurements reveal problems that bias, emotion and longevity cover up. If you have been doing your job for a long time without measurements, you might assume incorrectly that things are going well. (They may or may not be, but without measurements there is no way to tell.)

Improvement of supplier performance • Measurements identify whether suppliers are meeting your requirements. Do your suppliers know if your requirements are being met?

If you *cannot measure* an activity, you *cannot control* it. If you cannot control it, you *cannot manage* it. Without dependable measurements, intelligent decisions cannot be made.

Measuring is the act of assigning numbers to properties or characteristics. You measure to quantify a situation, to regulate or to understand what affects things you see. Sometimes you measure with gauges and instruments; sometimes you simply count things. Performance measures can help you understand and improve performance. It is exciting to measure, to benchmark and to stretch to do better.

Performance measurement systems are designed to allow the leaders of an organisation to link the vision to the execution of that vision. They provide a mechanism for assessing progress towards the vision.

Establishing a properly designed performance measurement system is a crucial step for many boardrooms if they are to fully understand the vital issue of shareholder value creation.[3] The board's hands are on some of the most powerful levers that can make managing for value a reality right down to the shop floor. These levers include ensuring that shareholder value creation is the paramount corporate objective; selecting and supporting the best CEO; approving the highest value corporate strategy; and assuring management incentives are aligned with those of shareholders.[4]

Some commentators argue that in Australia many boards still do not make use of these levers. The bottom line is that, despite all the rhetoric about the need to improve performance, the results so far suggest many companies simply talk about value creation strategies rather than act on them.[5] Such companies either fail to recognise, or are reluctant to implement, the sometimes painful and profound changes needed to achieve their goals in the face of structural changes that undermine competitiveness.

The fundamental purpose of performance measurement is to supply the key business performance drivers to the board so the directors can pull the right levers. Measurements, therefore, can be used for at least four purposes.

1. Control • Measurements help to reduce variation. For example, a manager of a company may have just signed a new contract with a shipping company which is offering significantly lower rates. The manager intends to pass through those cheaper rates to his clients because he realises that price is an important factor to them in the buy/do not buy decision. Measuring the delivery time of the new shipping carrier against the goal of 10% improvement over the year, or against the delivery time of the previous carrier, generically benchmarked against the delivery times of other, unrelated shipping carriers whose vessels leave the same loadport will provide the manager in question with key information for controlling the delivery time performance of the company against its client-oriented strategy.

2. Self-assessment • Measurements can be used to assess how your process is doing, including improvements that have been made.

3. Identify continuous improvement opportunities • Measurements can be used to identify defect sources, process trends, and stimulate action geared to defect prevention, and to determine process efficiency and effectiveness, as well as opportunities for improvement. Take the case of a company trying to improve the delivery time of its products. Suppose that it has a target this year of achieving a 10% improvement. If the measurement reports show that current delivery time is not improving but is steadily worsening, then the accountable manager can be alerted to the fact that a problem exists. This example indicates that where measurement reports are capable of preparation in a timely fashion, prompt corrective action can be taken.

4. Enhance management assessment • Without measurements there is no way to be certain you are meeting value-added objectives or that you are being effective and efficient. The basic concept of performance measurement involves:

(i)   planning and meeting established operating goals/standards;

(ii)   detecting deviations from planned levels of performance; and

(iii) restoring performance to the planned levels or achieving new levels of performance.

What you measure is what you manage. Suppose one of the client-oriented objectives of a company is to reduce total delivery time. In order to manage that, the company must devote resources to measure the key performance drivers of current delivery times. The objective in the first instance is to identify opportunities to facilitate process improvements, and secondly, to put in place those improvement initiatives so identified. Delivery time is how long it takes from the end of production until the product reaches the client. Without measuring delivery times, a company's managers limp along not really knowing if their delivery times are good, poor, getting worse, or superior to the delivery time of their toughest competitor. No manager whose role is held accountable over the processes which cumulatively drive the company's delivery time can make informed judgements about it. Nobody wins.

WHAT IS THE BASIS OF A PERFORMANCE MEASUREMENT SYSTEM?

Successful performance measurement systems adhere to the following principles:

▶   Measure only what is important. Do not measure too much; measure things that impact client satisfaction.

▶   Focus on client needs. Ask your clients if they think this is what you should measure.

- Involve employees in the design and implementation of the measurement system. Give them a sense of ownership. This improves the quality of the measurement system.

WHY CHANGE THE WAY WE MEASURE?

1. To become world class

You expect your organisation to become a world-class operator. The concept of what constitutes a world-class organisation changes as rapidly as markets change. In 1986 Schonberger defined world-class manufacturing as continuous and rapid improvement in such areas as quality, lead time and client service.[6] The problem with this definition is that many of the world-class organisations of the 1980s have shrunk in economic importance so much so that the definition cannot really be justified anymore. These organisations have clung to traditional performance measurement systems that just cannot deliver the requisite information.

Lochamy and Fox, on the other hand, view a world-class organisation as one whose client-based, internal business processes and finance functions synchronise their activities to achieve the corporate vision by meeting client's current and potential needs and expectations. A first step in becoming a world-class organisation is to understand the relationship between the primary business function (i.e. customer expectations, internal business processes, finance and learning, and growth functions).[7]

Similarly, Anderson Consulting (which examined the records of 50 world-class organisations) found that organisations have become world class by exploiting the following common characteristics:

▶ personal courageous leadership;
▶ commitment to the urgency for change;
▶ an obsession with client needs and expectations;
▶ insight into market discontinuities and the strategic implications;
▶ the development and exploitation of core competencies and key processes;
▶ pervasive behaviour change through participation and communication; and
▶ outcome-based measures to drive performance.[8]

TABLE 1   **Traditional and world-class organisations contrasted**

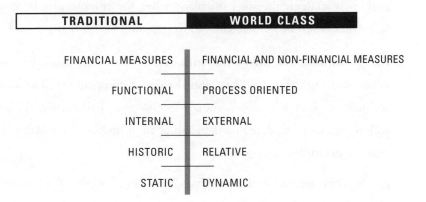

TRADITIONAL	WORLD CLASS
FINANCIAL MEASURES	FINANCIAL AND NON-FINANCIAL MEASURES
FUNCTIONAL	PROCESS ORIENTED
INTERNAL	EXTERNAL
HISTORIC	RELATIVE
STATIC	DYNAMIC

Table 1 compares the elements of a world-class organisation with a traditional organisation. Is your organisation closer to a traditional or world-class organisation?

2. To adjust to change

Competitive markets all over the world are changing. Unlike the 1970s and 1980s, the 1990s and beyond will test an organisation's ability to adapt and re-engineer itself over and over like never before. For example, during the 1980s the Hawke government recognised that public and private sector reform was a vital and necessary step for Australia's economic recovery. That recognition was the driving force behind the structural reconfiguration of the manufacturing industry (VDO Instruments Australia being a case in point), the deregulation of the Australian capital markets and the Wilenski reforms of the public sector.[9]

In 1994, the Karpin Report, *Enterprising Nation*, concluded that Australian management must improve significantly in the next decade if enterprises expect to even meet today's world best practice standards.[10] In particular, five forces have played a prominent role in effecting structural change in Australian industries.

i. Shifts in industry structure or product class life cycle. Demand for a product and the group of consumers that demand a product will change over a product's life. In the infancy stage of a product—when it is first introduced onto the market—competition centres around how innovative it is. As the market grows over time, when new competitors emerge and the industry becomes established, competition revolves around price, performance, service and quality.

ii. Competitive pressures. The emergence of competition into a market poses new strategic threats, particularly when the entrants play by new rules. Companies must be flexible enough to respond to such changes, and quickly.

iii. Technological advancements. The latest technological innovations always seem to change the established rules of competition. The absence of technology breeds complacency. Technology, particularly information technology, destabilises the market, and opens it up like never before, creating new opportunities in the process.

iv. Market peaks and troughs. The globalisation of all industries is changing the basis of competition. Organisations must realign their strategies inside the new world order. Exchange rates, stockmarkets around the world, oil, copper and aluminium prices, consumption patterns, interest rates, taxation and legal frameworks, deregulations, foreign ownership rules, tariffs, telecommunications and wars—these act as catalysts for change.

v. Growth. As organisations grow in size, they often find themselves the target in a takeover bid. Additionally, organisations—*really* successful ones—outgrow their original strategies. It is clear that strategies must change in order to facilitate further growth in the organisation.

3. To complement financial measures

Financial measures fall short in two ways. First, they do not capture all of an organisation's strategic objectives. Second, financial measures are lag indicators of performance. They answer the question 'How did we do?', and are collected after the event (i.e. provide information on outcomes). Non-financial measures, on the other hand, are mostly lead indicators of performance so that they answer the question 'How are we doing?' Accordingly, these measures are collected within the process and are forward looking and capable of providing diagnostic information to correct variation.

When designing non-financial measures, the intention is to design them so that they are lead indicators of performance. These measures are after-the-event measures of process outcomes, mostly quantification of client perceptions of outcomes, key process measures, aggregate measures of process outcomes, lead indicators of process outcomes, discrete measures of sub-process outcomes and lead indicators of sub-process outcomes.

Non-financial measures are used variously as a tool in continuous improvement programs. This includes driving priorities for improvement, monitoring perfor- mance improvement, assessing and monitoring end-to-end process performance and variation, and initiating the search for root causes of variation, by the people in the process to control the day-to-day operation of the process. Reporting on non- financial measures provides an early warning of things going wrong in the process so that corrective actions can be taken causing minimal overall profit impact.

Although financial measures are quantifiable, they are frequently difficult for non-accountants to understand. Softer measures, on the other hand, are predictive of client perceptions of process outcomes. Examples include customer perceptions of timeliness of service delivery, customer perceptions of relative value, total repair time, proportion of telephone book entries in error, time to take an order, and number of errors identified and corrected each hour.

To illustrate, Ford Motor Company in the United States, knowing that its Pinto was equipped with a petrol tank that was especially susceptible to damage and explosion in rear-end collisions, decided not to recall the car, reasoning that a recall would cost far more than the company was likely to lose in lawsuits by people who were maimed or killed in the relatively small number of explosions that could be foreseen as statistically likely to take place. Ford thought that by adopting the course of action which it did, its beloved bottom line would suffer relatively little impact from a few charred corpses.[11] Who can tell how differently Ford's executives may have acted had they considered the longer term impact on client satisfaction levels and brandname credibility before making their decision?

The point is that shareholders seek sustained profit growth *over the longer term*. For organisations listed on the Australian Stock Exchange, this is evidenced by real capital appreciation in the share price. For small businesses, it means selecting suppliers and clients with which to trade, developing trust and loyalty in these relationships, investing in your employees, equalling and surpassing client expectations and improving internal efficiencies.

Interpreting actions and events retrospectively, however, is quite different from affecting strategy prospectively. What managers want is information that links the corporate strategy to its execution.

Traditional Australian organisations believe in the canon 'If it ain't broken, leave it.' This practice can be inappropriate and dangerous.

The conditions which created and nurtured many of Australia's older organisations, such as BHP Ltd, were breathtakingly simple compared with the conditions facing organisations today. Organisations like BHP emerged at a time when the Australian population was rapidly expanding, and the stability of the economy was underpinned by the primary production industry. Moreover, their clients accepted the products and services they were given. Industry was either highly protected or tightly regulated and efficiency was simply not demanded.

Large Australian organisations have traditionally had tall organisational structures making it difficult for strategy to filter down the workforce. Small businesses either did not translate their vision into strategies, or, if they did, then it was not communicated to the people.[12]

In addition, Australian firms have faced structural barriers, such as:

▶ **psychological myopia.** Managers tend to view the world in ways that are psychologically comfortable and personally reassuring.

▶ **wasteful work patterns.** Evidenced by a tendency to shape one's activities so as to stay busy with familiar routines and avoid anxiety-provoking challenges.

▶ **performance expectations.** Managers avoid risk by asking their team members for less than is really possible or permitting them to escape from real commitments and consequences.

▶ **misuse of work management disciplines.** This explains the behaviour of employees to be casual, careless or cynical about work planning, measurement and tracking procedures.

▶ **the invisible conspiracy.** Being the underside of corporate culture is the unique tangle of debilitating patterns that are reinforced by formal and informal institutional mechanisms.[13]

In addition, the lack of accountability in the Australian business environment makes change difficult. Mr Frank Blount, former head of Telstra Corporation Limited said of organisations in 1998 that 'Nobody sticks their head up and everyone goes as a group, which means accountability is diffused and no-one is in charge of anything.'[14]

Even organisations that have seemingly beaten those structural barriers and actually design then implement a change program have performed poorly. Why? One reason is that the change program itself is insufficiently linked to the organisation's overall strategic plan. The change journey requires consensus on the current reality facing the organisation. The initiatives selected should be designed to take the organisation from its current reality and enable it to achieve its shared vision.[15]

SUMMARY

Performance measures focus the attention of your organisation on information. Naturally, some methods of using information to deliver improvements are more successful than others. Teamwork, co-operation, and openness are assets an organisation works to improve. Everyone wants to excel. Everyone wants to be part of a winning team. Too much zeal for results and accountability can lead to tampering and exactly the opposite effect you wish to produce. Few situations in the business world are entirely black and white. Education is required. Organisations need to decide what measures they need to be competitive and work to establish processes and systems that produce the desired results.

PART 2

THE NEED FOR AN INTEGRATED SYSTEM

Why your organisation needs a balanced scorecard

Turning off the autopilot
The balanced scorecard is a strategic management tool
Define your vision
Managing small businesses with the balanced scorecard
Unify your business
Promote innovative solutions
Link reward and compensation systems to performance measures
Focus the organisation on wealth creation

If we are strong, our strength will speak for itself.
If we are weak, words will be no help. JOHN F KENNEDY

Imagine a world in which you had the answers to the following four questions:

1. How do our clients see us?

2. What must we excel at?

3. How can we continue to create value?

4. How do we look to our shareholders?

Suppose *you knew* that most of your clients thought your products were great, but that your after-sales service was poor or non-existent and this was linked to low client loyalty, which in turn made your revenues volatile—then you would establish a better after-sales service to improve client satisfaction and revenue.

If you could identify the process inefficiency that was increasing the number of defects per 1000 units, you could improve the process or re-invent it before too many of your clients decided to walk.

You would be finally equipped with the information necessary to work out how productivity levels can be influenced by the level of cross–functional training your employees have, and avert potentially devastating consequences caused when too many of your employees are away sick at the same time.

Using a balanced scorecard, you can look at your business from four critical dimensions by complementing financial measures with performance measures for clients, internal business processes, and learning and growth actions. These measures differ significantly from those employed by many traditional organisations in one fundamental way: traditional organisations rely on operational and physical measures for local activities. These measures are *bottom up*. By contrast, the scorecard's measures are *top down*—derived from the organisation's strategic objectives and competitive demands.

TURNING OFF THE AUTOPILOT

The scorecard allows you to focus attention on four critical areas of the business. Central to this is the notion that time is a valuable commodity and it is something you do not have enough of. You want to know as much as you can about your organisation without sensory saturation at the same time. How many times has your organisation generated reports containing excessive numbers of measures, many of which you doubt are necessary? Several, no doubt. What seems to happen is that organisations allow the performance measurement system to evolve in a piecemeal and ad hoc way—redolent of the way in which tax legislation has developed in Australia. The balanced scorecard centralises the performance measurement system by focusing on a handful of measures that are most critical to the organisation.

Accordingly, the balanced scorecard meets a number of managerial needs. First, the scorecard reports centrally via a single report all of the organisation's separate arms of the business such as: improving product quality, shortening response times, emphasising team work and cross-functionalism, reducing manufacturing cycle times and new product time to market and managing for the long term.

The scorecard is like an insurance policy against sub-optimisation. By reporting all of the elements of the business together on a single scorecard, managers can see how a change of one element would impact on other elements of the organisation.

The balanced scorecard drives financial performance. Developed originally by Kaplan and Norton, it proved a powerful strategic framework that can yield a different, richer interpretation of actions and events than other frameworks have been able to. The essence of the balanced scorecard is that it is able to provide decision makers with a comprehensive framework that translates an organisation's strategic objectives into a coherent set of performance measures. The scorecard is more than just another measurement exercise. It is a strategic management system that can motivate breakthrough improvements in key business areas like client satisfaction rates, product quality levels, process efficiencies and employee development. And it does so without eliminating the use of financial measures. It *complements* them with non-financial, key operational measures.

The scorecard is *balanced* because it emphasises competing aspects of an organisation in ways that augment the organisation's capacity to adapt to changing competitive markets in the pursuit of competitive strategy. That the scorecard is balanced is significant in two regards. It suggests that no single measure is 'perfect' and that a search for one is pointless, perhaps even counterproductive. Balance implies that an organisation's measurement set fits neatly with what it is trying to achieve. This concept is illustrated by Table 2.

For example, National Westminster Bank, one of the largest banking institutions in the United Kingdom, is having to contend with growing competition. In the context of performance measurement this has been greatest in

TABLE 2   **The balanced scorecard: the four dimensions**

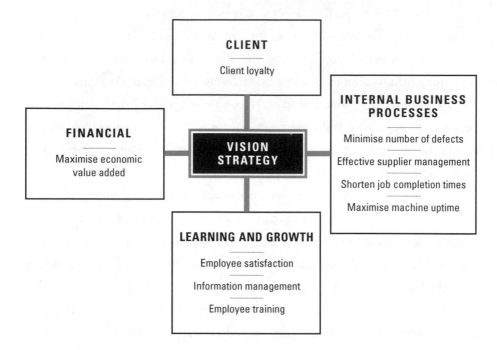

terms of technology developments, management changes and financial results. NatWest has adopted the balanced scorecard approach and found that it has added significant value by focusing on business processes, client satisfaction, business results and organisational development. The scorecard is now being extended to all major areas of the business.[16]

Evaluating the actual performance of an organisation against its strategy is not an easy task. The balanced scorecard simplifies the process. For instance, if a large cargo vessel can transport over 500 containers from port to port, then not only must all of the containers be fitted and securely fastened for the voyage, the ship master must navigate across wide open sea, often through violent tempests, ensuring all the while that the containers—and their precious cargo—remain intact. The master's instruments must be operational and alternative pathways must be constructed in the event something goes wrong. The point is that many factors affect an organisation's performance and that to successfully navigate an organisation into the next millennium its leaders must be briefed constantly on all of the key measures affecting its performance.

Organisations can benefit from deploying a balanced scorecard in many ways. This chapter will critically assess several of them. The perceived benefits of the balanced scorecard that will be assessed are listed below, in the order in which they appear in the chapter:

- ▶ the balanced scorecard is a strategic management tool;
- ▶ small businesses can derive many benefits not previously available to them;
- ▶ unification of business;
- ▶ promote innovative solutions;
- ▶ complement financial measures;
- ▶ strengthen communication lines;
- ▶ link reward and compensation systems to performance measures; and
- ▶ focus the organisation on wealth creation.

THE BALANCED SCORECARD IS A STRATEGIC MANAGEMENT TOOL

Your organisation needs a scorecard so that you can manage performance strategically. Frustrated by the inadequacies of traditional performance measurement systems, many organisations have abandoned financial measures of performance. Why? 'Make operational improvements and the numbers will follow' the argument goes. But well-trained managers do not want to choose between financial and operational measures. Managers want a balanced presentation of measures that allows them to view the organisation from several key dimensions simultaneously.

Successful organisations are implementing the balanced scorecard as a combined strategic measurement and management system. The results have been astounding and have left little doubt that, starting now, the balanced scorecard will become a standard strategic management practice.

Putting forward a case for supporting the balanced scorecard, Alan Jones says that in 1996 Ericsson Australia—a world-class telecommunications company—won a coveted Australian Quality Award, and he credits the scorecard system with a portion of that success. He also points to sales growth of two-and-a-half times the figure of three years ago. He cannot credit the balanced scorecard with the growth in the overall telecommunications market but puts the case that Ericsson's market share of that growth is traceable to internal factors.[17]

Promote organisational alignment

The balanced scorecard should contain all important strategic, financial, client, product and service, people and process goals. These can be deployed throughout the organisation, creating a strong degree of organisational alignment, providing the basis for comprehensive sets of local measures, and linking measures up, down and across the organisation. A fully deployed balanced scorecard should:

▶ balance financial with non-financial measures;

▶ be solidly grounded in the voice of the client;

▶ clarify what needs to be measured;

▶ drive measurement through the organisation;

▶ focus attention on the few critical issues facing the organisation;

▶ help the organisation guard against the proliferation of unneeded or wasteful measures;

▶ identify strategic objectives;

▶ link measures throughout the organisation;

▶ promote organisational alignment; and

▶ reduce measurement anxiety by demystifying the subject.

In summary, the balanced scorecard is a system of critical measurements for an organisation. It exists in recognition of the fact that financial results are the most lagging of indicators and that the primary components of organisational health should be tracked. The balanced scorecard shows how results are achieved and provides a linked system of short-term (goals) and long-term (vision) indicators to help managers manage people and processes and to help people manage their own work.[18]

A new tool for every manager

This new approach arms managers with a set of performance measures which collectively capture the complete corporate strategy to help power forward the business. The measures themselves more clearly define managers' focus and, importantly, their accountabilities to all of the corporate capabilities required to realise an organisation's ultimate business vision. Each of the four questions posed earlier balance manager's attention across the four dimensions of the business:

At last managers have the ultimate tool to deliberately reconfigure the organisation by focusing and directing the attention of the entire firm to the performance

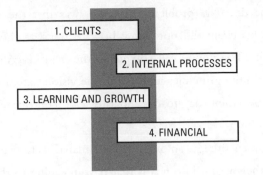

measures (and necessarily all of the things that must be changed to improve them) to unleash all of the organisation's creative energies.

It signals the end of the static, rigid, ill-equipped performance measurement system of a by-gone era. It is dynamic and fluid. It adapts in line with shifts in the business strategy, be they minor modifications or major overhauls. The scorecard provides a basis for setting long-term performance objectives, which drive performance improvements.

DEFINE YOUR VISION

If an organisation's vision is not translated into definable terms satisfactorily, then it can have disastrous effects on the whole organisation. Take the case of Candela Laser. Its poorly translated strategy was blamed for the retrenchment of 30 of its staff. Analysts said Candela failed to upgrade products, invested too much money in an ophthalmic laser that flopped, and got walloped by a competitor (run by its own founder, Horace W. Furumoto) that offered dermatological lasers that were 50% cheaper.[19]

Then there is the instance of the managing director of a steel manufacturing company who, after working with his management team for several months to develop a vision statement, received an email from one of his sales manager's in the field. The manager said, 'I fully believe in our vision statement but my clients do not understand it. I tried to explain it to them, but frankly, I cannot understand it either.'

That company's vision statement, like those of so many other companies, declared an intention to 'deliver client service excellence to provide services that surpass clients' needs'. The problem, however, was that the sales manager, his support staff and his client did not know how to translate those words into the appropriate actions. The phone call convinced the managing director that a large gap existed between the principles inherent in the vision statement and employees' knowledge of how their day-to-day actions can contribute to realising the company's vision.

The scorecard encourages an organisation's managers to reach a consensus and then to translate their vision into terms that have meaning to the employees who would realise the vision.

Translating the vision is a process that enables the leaders to temporarily put aside reason and look beyond the present to the future as they would like to see it. Having the mentality 'it cannot be done' is irrelevant and should be avoided. Turning your vision into reality can only happen after your vision has been created. A vision must be leader initiated, shared and supported, comprehensive and detailed, and inspiring.

A vision statement should be clear, brief and succinct, broad and evolving in nature, but not so broad that it becomes meaningless. Self-supporting is how several comentators have described it. It should exhibit some real stretch. All of the words used in the vision should be specific and purposeful.

One Tasmanian clothes manufacturer has used the balanced scorecard to translate its vision. Its new vision now reads 'Our mission is to provide services, support and products to all clients. We work cooperatively, seek continuous improvement and innovation and interact with others, so that we are models for all employees.'

Align your vision and its tactical execution

The balanced scorecard is perhaps the best means available to gain consistent alignment between a board's strategic vision and its tactical execution. The balanced scorecard helps organisations move from being financially driven to mission driven.[20]

Clarify your strategies

The efficiencies associated with the scorecard are compelling. It is an effective means for clarifying the business strategy and for improving communication at all levels of the organisation. The scorecard by its very nature, forces managers to reach consensus on the ultimate business intent. It sets directions in a straight-shooting fashion. Moreover, the four-pronged approach to the scorecard allows managers to see, quite often for the first time, how their decisions affect other corporate organs.

Evaluate and control the strategic plan

Once you have designed and implemented your balanced scorecard, managers must evaluate the strategic plan to ensure that the corporate objectives have been met. The strategic plan defines the organisation's overall mission and objectives. Within each business unit, functional plans must be prepared. In many cases, this process simply means a revamp of the financials. The problem is that the strategic plan traditionally contains only financial data, and it is hardly ever used by managers as the benchmark against which to compare the monthly and quarterly reports.

Now you can integrate the strategic planning, annual planning and quarterly forecast processes by a process of setting long-range corporate goals and setting targets. The outcome is an annual plan that supports the business strategies. Consider the process outline in Table 3.

Detailed financial planning remains important, but now your organisation has an integrated planning process that specifically incorporates the three other balanced scorecard dimensions. In an integrated planning process the role of the annual plan is modified to *complement* short-term financial performance with short-term targets for measures in the client, internal business process, and continuous improvement dimensions. With the link between vision and its tactical execution firmly in place, you can safely test the assumptions underpinning the strategy and the strategy's execution.

TABLE 3 **Strategic planning process**

| GOALS | MEASURES | TARGETS | INITIATIVES |

STRATEGIC PLAN

ANNUAL PLAN

QUARTERLY FORECAST

At the end of a scorecard strategic planning process, you should have set targets for each long-term critical success factor for each scorecard dimension. In addition, they should have identified the improvement plans necessary to support the objectives and have allocated resources to those plans.

Improve goal setting

Changing the behaviour of the workforce requires more than awareness of corporate goals. How can your organisation's strategic objectives and measures be translated in a way that is meaningful for business units, teams and individuals?

A large mining company has developed a technique to enable and encourage individuals to set goals in consultation with their line managers that are concordant with the company's goals. It has created an on-line personal scorecard that employees can access each time they log on to the computer. The scorecard contains four layers of information. The first layer sets out the corporate objectives, measures and targets. The second translates corporate targets into targets for each business unit. The third layer translates business unit targets into targets for each division. For the fourth layer, the employee inputs his own targets that are consistent with the division's targets.

The on-line scorecard assists the company in communicating its corporate and business unit objectives to all of the employees, thereby enabling the company to translate those objectives into meaningful tasks and targets for all employees.

Enhance employee motivation

While the balanced scorecard is getting a warm reception from the likes of operations executives and vice presidents of sales and marketing, quality and planning, the approach is more popular with top corporate managers and directors.

The balanced scorecard helps teams develop focus and effectiveness by creating their own measures and feedback systems. In turn, this builds employee under-standing, support and commitment to attaining targeted levels of performance.

Accordingly, the scorecard is a valuable vehicle for driving workforce motivation improvements. To the extent that an organisation can realise those benefits, it steers away from the dangerous course of tracking everything that moves (or at least measures which do not of themselves drive the numbers that form part of the bottom line). And properly implemented, a scorecard can add value to the corporate balance sheet by eliminating wasteful non-value-adding work altogether, thereby freeing up valuable resources for more critical tasks.

Promote learning

The scorecard is specifically designed to increase an organisation's ability to change its measures in line with shifts in the strategic intent and the goals of the entity. This can occur through a process of single and double loop learning.

Single loop learning

Defining the vision, communicating and linking, and scorecard strategic planning are not sufficient of themselves to stay in control of strategic change. Those tools are important single loop learning processes—*single loop* in the sense that organisations compare their performances to a set of pre-established standards and try to make appropriate adjustments. A single loop management process does not require the organisation to re-evaluate its strategy or the techniques used to implement it in light of current conditions.

You can test the validity of the cause and effect relationships between the key performance measures, goals and targets. For example, Mouse About Plc, a British software distributor (not its real name), had a balanced scorecard in place for over 18 months and as part of the bi-annual review sought to test the validity of the cause-and-effect relationships that existed in its scorecard. Mouse About Plc measured the correlation between measures in *different* dimensions.

The results of the review found significant positive correlations between employees' morale (a measure in the learning and growth dimension) and less defective products (an important internal business process dimension measure). Staff training resulted in less product defects, which was traced to shorter product delivery times, which in turn produced a stronger client-based relationship that led to higher levels of client satisfaction and lower working capital. A lower working capital meant a higher internal rate of return and a better earnings per share in the marketplace, which sustained market interest in the stock. The company also found correlations between research and development expenditures as a percentage of sales and the gross margin from new product sales, and between employee training hours and complaint resolution times.

The existence of such correlations confirm the company's business strategy from a single loop learning perspective. If Mouse About failed to find the existence of positive correlations by the time it conducted the review, it would be prudent to consider the assumptions underpinning the business' strategy.

For large organisations, multinationals, public sector utilities and the like, gathering enough information to track correlations between some or all of the different measures may take a long time and care must be taken to monitor the level of resources being consumed.

Double loop learning

Many organisations today face highly competitive environments of a fluid and dynamic nature. New opportunities and threats emerge seemingly overnight, and new players appear across the board. Firms facing torrid times may question the value of building their own balanced scorecard—after all, the strategy may not even be relevant by the time the scorecard is complete.

Your organisation must become capable of *double loop learning*—which requires that you periodically reassess standards themselves to ensure that these are relevant. In this way, the balanced scorecard can be used as a tool to reassess the strategies of the organisation in line with market shifts.

Strategic learning

The balanced scorecard allows firms to engage in strategic learning. *Strategic learning* embraces a formal process of linking the work of all employees' roles to the organisation's purpose, gathering feedback, testing the assumptions on which strategies are based then making the requisite adjustments. It is demonstrated in Table 4. Table 4 shows that for an organisation where the work of employees' roles are linked to the vision statement, metrics data can confirm whether the *vision* is

TABLE 4   **Strategic learning model**

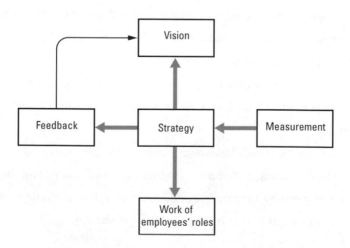

right or wrong. From then on, the organisation can reconfigure its vision statement, objectives, goals, targets and improvement initiatives to put things back on track.

The scorecard offers a design infrastructure which impliedly supports strategic learning in two ways:

1. By articulating the purpose of the organisation and then translating it into strategic objectives for each of the four dimensions that are understood by everybody in the organisation, the balanced scorecard successfully aligns the work of everybody's roles to the shared vision.

2. The scorecard shifts the focus of managers away from past performance to the validity of the firm's current strategies. In traditional firms senior managers and executives typically meet monthly to discuss the performance of the company or business unit over the last quarter. Questions raised more often than not focus on the reasons why the company or business unit has failed to meet its planned financial objectives for the period. In firms using the balanced scorecard, the managers who meet to analyse the company's results for a period can evaluate the validity of the company or business unit's strategy and the quality of its execution. If the performance indicators are well below the targets for that point in time, then senior managers are immediately aware that the assumptions underpinning the firm's strategy may be no longer valid.

You can then collectively weigh up market conditions, competitors' behaviour and the political environment. From that review, the managers may make a judgement to affirm, vary or revoke the current strategy. In any event, the balanced scorecard is a valid tool to hold managers accountable for their decision making against the backdrop of the corporate strategy. This capability for organisational learning at the senior tiers of an organisation adds value to the balanced scorecard as a strategic management tool.

In addition, the strategic plan, the annual plan and other financially based tools are single loop measures only. World-class organisations can use the balanced scorecard to assist their managers to make their assessment of the organisation's standards by questioning first the strategy then the 'flow on' factors. By contrast, traditional firms use tools like the annual plan to adjust 'flow on' factors without first testing the business case for the assumptions underpinning the strategy. If this paragraph was about the 100 metre sprint, it would be easy to tell which sprinter would win the race.

The second reason why your business should follow the scorecard approach applies to small businesses. Small businesses which adopt the balanced scorecard approach can derive many successes not previously available to them. Traditional small businesses measure performance using financial metrics only. World-class small companies, on the other hand, can use three *additional* means to measure company performance by asking the following questions:

▶ How do clients see us?

▶ What must we excel at?

▶ How can we continue to improve and create value?

Consideration of these areas allows translation of a company's vision into each of the four constituent dimensions of the balanced scorecard, giving stakeholders greater ability to:

▶ control costs;

▶ build employee understanding, support and commitment to attaining targeted performance levels; and

▶ lead the organisation by changing employee recognition and reward systems.

Consider, for example, a mechanical repair shop concerned about the level of client satisfaction. The shop's managers should be measuring key performance enablers relating to clients, such as the percentage of error-free jobs, number of quotes compared with jobs successfully completed, average size of accounts, percentage of new against old business (using records dating back at least 12 months) and age of client relationships to determine the level of client satisfaction.

In this way, the company's attention will be drawn to opportunities for improvement which could then be exploited. For example, a mechanic tracks the client satisfaction rate and finds improvement in one area (tune-ups) but reduction in another (tyre repairs and wheel alignments). The mechanic is then asked to identify the causes: are the factors non-systematic (e.g. winter is approaching) or systematic (such as a specialist tyre fitting outfit has opened nearby, or a competitor is advertising new lower prices)?

Some commentators also suggest there is value in tracking the number and type of client complaints received by the small business per month. Arguably, this could help determine whether a pattern exists, and assist in improving processes in areas where clients consistently complain, such as job completion time.

Although each business is unique and must identify its own internal issues, there are some useful generic performance measures. These include measuring the time between job completion and the booking date, and time between the billing and payment dates, and client call response times.

Learning and growth

If a small business is to turn into a learning organisation, it must encourage learning and growing thus advocating the continuous testing of experience and the transformation of that experience into knowledge accessible to all employees. No firm—big or small—can achieve and maintain world-class status without continually reappraising its situation for new opportunities.

Consider, in relation to the mechanical repair shop, the level of usage of old parts and paint left after previous repairs. Knowing who is using those parts and paint relative to the number of cars of that type and colour coming through the door will assist in determining whether employees are inflating costs unnecessarily. If the utilisation rate proves to be low, then emphasis should be made on the use of and value in turning over old parts; then measure whether usage increases.

Shaw Contracting, a Tasmanian business with fewer than 50 employees, advocates SWOT analysis (Strengths, Weaknesses, Opportunities, Threats) of the company's competitive position. Shaw identified about 70 areas that needed improvement, such as becoming accredited as approved tenderers with Tasmania's transport department.

Another important measure is the company's rate of training and employee development. Consideration of the company's planned expenditure for re-training employees in areas such as client service skills is essential.

To truly gauge improvement in the ability of a small business to be a learning organisation, an internal survey is required regularly. A firm could survey employee attitudes to the organisation semi-annually, asking each person to give a score of their feelings about various aspects of the business. If the firm is small enough, the survey could be carried out informally throughout the year.

One tool-maker company, AS Tools, is measuring its processes as part of its continuous improvement method of management. It monitors performance from three dimensions: financial, client and internal business processes. AS Tools believes quarterly financial indicators alone do not provide all the information needed to make sound decisions, so it has sought to broaden reporting parameters.

Key drivers measured on the financial front include contribution margin per machine, contribution margin per job, metal wastage costs and ageing rates. The firm has also established goals defining achievable rates of performance over one-, two- and five-year time horizons.

AS Tools monitors the number of client complaints it receives and logs each one by type (e.g. whether it relates to billing), machine downtime and employee absences. Measuring machine downtime helped establish it was more profitable to have one less machine on the floor. That machine was sold, creating valuable floorspace and eliminating unnecessary lease repayments.

Since 1995, AS Tools has tracked the cash receipts from its top 10 clients. The owner believes this information is a valuable indicator of client satisfaction levels. That is particularly the case when the client is financially healthy.

To respond to client concerns, AS Tools implemented a client management system. One person manages all elements of the client relationship and all aspects of a job. Each person's duties are in writing so employees know what is expected. There is much to be said for giving control of systems to the employees, thus creating a sense of ownership.

Guidelines

A company will not survive unless it knows how to achieve a competitive advantage in the marketplace. Managers of small firms might think that only the blue-chip companies need strategic measurement systems and balanced scorecards. The reality is, however, that every company has to know how to equal and surpass its competitors. Small business owners have a number of tools to measure key processes, and these include using a simple balanced scorecard and finding three or four critical processes to measure from each of the four dimensions.

Measuring critical processes in a firm presupposes that the proprietors want continuous improvement. There is no value in measuring performance if the information is not used to make operational improvements. Tracking the drivers of performance is a tool to enable business to focus on the future.

De-emphasising the cashflow and profit and loss statements is an efficient way to change current mindsets. To bring about a shift in behaviour, greater links to client's needs are required.

Despite objections from those who prefer the status quo, there is a good deal of anecdotal evidence that measures of quality and client satisfaction are finally beginning to affect small businesses across the board. Although hundreds of multinational businesses, such as Ericsson Australia, Toyota, Motorola, and IBM, have already incorporated continuous improvement principles and methods into their business, small business operators are just now beginning to explore the tremendous possibilities.

For small businesses that accept the value of the balanced scorecard, there are some useful guidelines:

▶ **Decide who will determine what to measure**. Should it be one of the directors? The accountant? The personal assistant? A combination of these.

Once this is settled, that person must determine what the company wants to measure. This can be done by reference to a mission statement or by considering the company's aims. The vision of the firm must be defined to the extent practicable into each of the four dimensions so that the measures selected enable the business to pull on the right levers.

▶ **Set goals**. After the processes have been measured for a few months and the current performance level has been determined, a series of goals of improved performance should be established. To help determine a goal, ask clients or other non-competing firms about their standard for performance.

▶ **Avoid overload**. The processes to be gauged should be measurable and controllable. Trying to track too many variables or processes that are driven by external circumstances can detract from actual business activity. It might be worth starting off with two or three processes to measure in each of the four areas identified by the balanced scorecard.

If the business has a number of branches or outlets, it might be good to measure the same process in each one. If one branch is consistently outperforming another, then the store managers could compare notes and see how the process differed in each area.

▶ **Stay objective**. Managers should be careful to avoid using measurement results to attack employees' performance; results are to give feedback and help the business grow. The issue of who will see the performance measurement results should be decided beforehand: are the results shared with the entire firm or only with those people involved in the process that's being measured?

These guidelines are flexible and adaptable, and are meant to enhance the use of the balanced scorecard by small businesses. The objective for the managers of small firms is to ultimately improve the bottom line. The key point to remember is that what gets measured, gets managed.

UNIFY YOUR BUSINESS

The balanced business scorecard brings together on a single management report many of the disparate elements of an organisation's competitive agenda.[21] It forces senior managers to consider all the important operational measures together, letting them see whether an improvement in one area was achieved at the expense of another. For example, reducing the time to market can be achieved in two different ways: by improving the management of new product introductions or by releasing products that are incrementally different from existing products.[22]

PROMOTE INNOVATIVE SOLUTIONS

Senior managers naturally gravitate toward financial measures because they provide consistent comparisons across an organisation and offer multi-year views of performance. But with the business scorecard senior managers are empowered to think in softer, non-financial terms where they historically have not placed much emphasis. The new ways of thinking that evolve promote new solutions to age old problems.

COMPLEMENT FINANCIAL MEASURES

The value of non-financial measures comes from their flexibility. They are just-in-time tools that can be focused on specific problem conditions, such as service lapses.

You can change the measures as problems are solved, or as the measures lose their punch. For executives who can overcome their uneasiness with new measurement systems, a timely payoff may be in store.

STRENGTHEN COMMUNICATION LINES

The purpose of the scorecard is to translate strategy into measures that uniquely communicate your vision across the organisation.[23] Open participation in developing a balanced scorecard is a longer process and probably more expensive. Nevertheless, it can offer a number of advantages: input from a larger pool of talent is incorporated into the internal objectives; lower-level managers develop a greater understanding of the organisation's longer term strategic objectives than what might otherwise be the case; and input from a larger group simplifies the buy-in process. But getting the thumbs up from managers early on in the piece is only one step in linking individual actions to corporate goals.

The balanced scorecard signals to everyone what the organisation is trying to achieve for all stakeholders. However, to align the work of employees' roles with the corporate strategy, the balanced scorecard users should set goals and link compensation systems to performance measures.

LINK REWARD AND COMPENSATION SYSTEMS TO PERFORMANCE MEASURES

How can you lead your organisation through a significant change in the way that employees and teams are measured and rewarded? The scorecard marries up incentives with the organisation's intentions.

Should compensation systems be linked to balanced scorecard measures? Compensation systems are the framework within which managers give recognition to each employee in their team in accordance with an assessment of their individual work performance in such a way that the assessment and the reasons for it are open to review. Some organisations have been quick to take the view that linking employees' compensation to performance measures more closely aligns the work of people's roles to the organisation's goals, and these organisations have been just as quick to rewrite their performance appraisal systems. By way of illustration, an Australian mining company ties 25% of its executives' bonuses to their achievement of ambitious targets in respect of a weighted average 'basket' of three financial measures: internal rate of return, earnings per share and cash flow. Another 25% of salary is based on soft indicators like client satisfaction and continuous improvement initiatives in place.

The fluid nature of early balanced scorecards makes many organisations reluctant to put real teeth in their new system. Kaplan of Harvard Business School has said that this is as it should be. In his view, organisations should treat their initial scorecard as an hypothesis, a theory of the business. You want your employees to participate with you in the learning process. If you link incentives to the scorecard in the early stages, then they will assume you got the measures right and they'll maximise along those dimensions.[24]

Without the tie to compensation, organisations run the risk of sending the wrong signals to employees. How can you ask people to pay attention to operational performance and yet give bonuses only for financials?

One solution can be found in Cigna Insurance's property and casualty division, which began managing its business with a scorecard at the start of 1995. Today, bonuses which constitute as much as 10 % of management and employee compensation packages are tied completely to scorecard results. Financial performance is still the most important determinant of bonuses and counts for 50 % of the bonus.

Cigna defends this approach on the basis that it is better for an organisation to feel its way through a new experience than jump head-on into a black hole. The division is putting in a new performance measurement system, a new strategic system and a new compensation system—all at the same time. So they have decided to iterate to the final outcome rather than get there in one giant leap.

Shoebridge has recently stated that two of the central changes for compensation in Australian industry will be defensive salary packaging to lessen the effect of the superannuation surcharge on contributions by higher income earners. This also applies to executives who place larger portions of their incomes at risk by linking their salaries to performance. [25]

Opportunities are opening up for high performers to negotiate a bigger tax-effective pay. In 1992, only 50% of senior executives received performance-linked packages compared with 90% in 1997. In the next two years, Shoebridge claims that incentive payments will go to 95% of senior management (constituting up to half their pay), 75% of middle management (a third) and 50% of supervisory staff (a quarter).

Admittedly though, most organisations have sat on the sideline, either waiting to see if the stance taken by the few proactive firms pays off, or because they are still working through the issues. Time will tell. As for the questions executives should be thinking about in relation to the design of their scorecard:[26]

▶ Are the information systems capable of delivering the right information so that the work performance appraisal process can be fair?

▶ Could unintended and negative consequences ensue as a direct result of the manner in which the targets for the measures are achieved?

▶ Will the scorecard have the right measures on it?

▶ What are the legal implications for the organisation if the scorecard does not have the right measures on it so that the appraisal is unfair or that commercially the business suffers from the way a target is achieved?

In addition, traditional organisations have incorporated numerous objectives into the compensation formula by weighting each objective and calculating incentive compensation by the extent to which each weighted objective is achieved. In many instances, organisations incorporate into the formula a 'market adjustment' which may be applied to cope with market conditions applying from time to time for roles requiring specific skills.

That the balanced scorecard has a role to play in the determination of incentive compensation is clear. Precisely what that role should be will become clearer as more organisations experiment with linking rewards to scorecard measures.

FOCUS THE ORGANISATION ON WEALTH CREATION

The final reason for adopting the balanced scorecard approach is based on the notion that a balanced scorecard gets the organisation focused. The target is wealth creation, and the bulls-eye is strategy. It aims continuously for the bulls–eye, which should mean a reduction in the level of side-tracking of managers. In a very direct way, the scorecard allows an organisation's people to gather momentum to force improvements to the processes underpinning the measures in the execution of the corporate intent.

SUMMARY

Organisations choose to adopt balanced scorecards for a number of reasons. The scorecard applies equally to large organisations as it does to small businesses. The scorecard has a role to play in articulating strategy, communicating strategy across the organisation, aligning every employees' roles with the strategy, and conducting systematic performance reviews to learn about and improve strategy.

The cause-and-effect relationships between the measures mean that a change in one area of the model will reinforce earlier changes made elsewhere. Therefore, each change made by managers over the life of the scorecard cumulatively add to the momentum that keeps the organisation moving in the desired direction.

AN INTEGRATED SYSTEM — THE BALANCED SCORECARD

How do our clients see us?

I am easily satisfied with the very best. WINSTON CHURCHILL

You can always tell world-class organisations from traditional ones: world-class organisations focus on their clients. They do this to retain clients, to win new ones and to protect long-term profits. A client focus can make the whole organisation receptive. While many organisations today espouse the importance of client satisfaction, far fewer exhibit excellence in their client satisfaction-related activities. This is true both in measurement and implementation. Client satisfaction is about more than just keeping clients happy. It is about setting a standard of excellence and delighting clients through superior performance.[27] This chapter examines why organisations must focus on their clients and measure the key perspectives of value for them. Also considered are the readjustment issues organisations must face once they find that their mission statements are not aligned with clients' expectations. Of course, the chapter would not be complete without a comprehensive treatment on measuring client complaints, identifying client-focused measures and a brief discussion of how to measure.

WHY FOCUS ON YOUR CLIENTS?

By focusing on your clients you can help your organisation to target its priorities and expenditures, plan strategically, improve productivity and efficiency, and rationalise its services and operations. Of course, you do not lay red carpets for your clients for nothing; you do it because you expect to make a profit. Porter has said that creating value for buyers that exceeds the cost of doing so is the goal of any generic strategy.

Mission statements are about leadership and vision. Those that use words like 'commitment' and 'honesty' and talk of looking after customers and employees recall Napoleon Bonaparte's famous line: 'An army marches on its stomach'. In other words, if you do not look out for the people who buy your products or services (and the people who work for you), you will lose. For example, Australian and New Zealand computer giant Honeywell Limited, which in 1997 won an Australian Quality award, changed dramatically since 1994. The company moved from a hierarchical management structure to one that is flat and team based. This lead to increased sales and revenue and far closer relationships with major clients.

For the avoidance of doubt on the importance of a client-oriented strategy, look at what happens to an organisation which does not have a strategy:

> *On average, the CEOs of US corporations lose half their customers every five years. This fact shocks most people. It shocks the CEOs themselves, many of whom have little insight into the causes of this customer exodus, let alone the cures, because they do not measure customer defections, make little effort to prevent them, and fail to use defections as a guide to improvements.*[28]

Your organisation has a vision or mission statement because you want your employees to know how their role fits in relation to the purpose of the organisation. In particular, vision statements exist so that your clients know what you hope to achieve, where you are heading, how you intend to get there and what principles you value.

With the balanced scorecard, you can empower your staff to translate each and every element of the mission statement into specific performance measures so that you can really measure the factors that count to your clients. This idea is represented graphically by Table 5. The assumption here is that the mission statement accurately reflects what *is* in fact important to your clients. (Regrettably, that is often not the

TABLE 5   **Client dimension**

Balanced Scorecard
DIMENSIONS AND OBJECTIVES

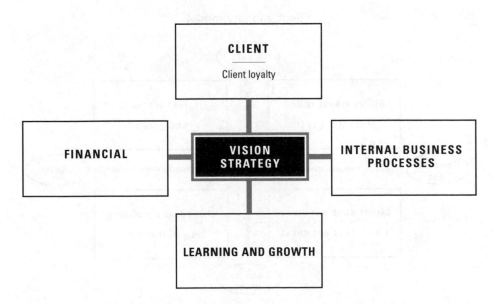

case.) The scorecard can track measures concerning client satisfaction, loyalty and market share.

The balanced scorecard system can apply to large or small firms, manufacturing or service firms, joint venture arrangements, even businesses that rely on virtual clients. In every case, the principles underlying the balanced scorecard remain valid. Client's concerns generally fall into three discrete categories: time, performance and service, and price. Have a look at Table 6 to see where your organisation fits in the Client Window Model.

Lawrence Crosby says of the myth 'what you measure is what you change' that whilst this may be true in physics, it is not so in client satisfaction. He remarks that some organisations have had a client satisfaction measurement program in place for years, but have produced no results in terms of improved bottom-line profits. Instead, he says they only see a flat line. The problem is that such organisations have assumed measurement was necessary and sufficient for change. But client satisfaction requires a deployment plan. A full commitment means that everyone in the organisation knows who their clients are and has targets, plans and measures established for improving client satisfaction.[29] The next section looks at what clients value.

TABLE 6 **Client window model**

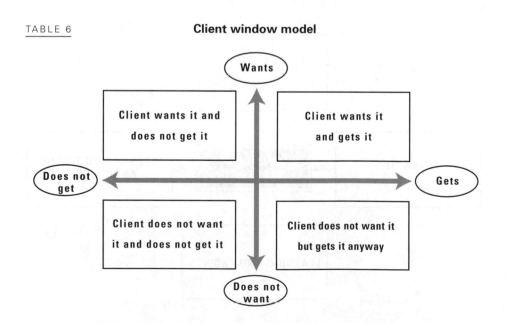

MEASURING THE KEY PERSPECTIVES OF VALUE FOR CLIENTS

1 Time

Time impacts clients in a number of ways. The cycle time from the point when the client places an order to its ultimate delivery and the variance of that cycle time impact the client's business immediately. To illustrate, the speed and reliability of an organisation to respond to client orders can provide significant value to clients through their holding lower inventory levels and less working capital, and allowing quicker response by them to *their* clients. Using the balanced scorecard supports the way organisations can handle information and the strength of their ties to the clients' business.

2 Performance and service

Performance and service are related concepts concerning what a product or service does for a client and how well it does it. The combination of performance and service measure how a company's products or services contribute to creating value for its clients. The giant New York bank, Chemical Bank, realised that it had to measure the key drivers of its performance so that it could in turn improve client satisfaction. *USA Today* reported Chemical Bank's bright idea on August 16 1988 like this:

> *Chemical Bank clients are playing Beat the Clock—and losing. The giant New York City Bank is paying $5 to clients who have to wait more than seven minutes at its busiest branches in midtown Manhattan and the Wall Street area. 'Clients tend to remember when they wait. This helps them remember when they don't', says Chemical's Ken Herz. Clients watch a digital clock in the bank lobby to time how long they're kept waiting. So far, the bank is winning. It has given out an average of $5 a week at each branch.*

Performance and service includes the quality of products and services, the consistency of their performance, their functionality, serviceability and their appearance. Quality measures the percentage of defective products delivered to a client and the time it takes to deliver those orders. By discovering features of performance and service that are valued by the clients you can set agendas for systematic improvements that can be the key to achieving business goals.

The ongoing provision of performance and service does not depend on invention. Usually, excellence in this area depends on relentless, systematic, target-oriented work in continuously improving processes.

3. Price

Price is the most immediate basis of competition in the short and long term. This is nowhere more evident than in the retail petroleum industry. When was the last time you ditched a petrol company for another one on the basis of the quality of the petrol or diesel you bought? Price takes on particular importance where there is little opportunity to differentiate a product or service at the generic level. Talking of price, James Anderson and James Narus have put it this way:

> *What are your products and services actually worth to customers? Remarkably few suppliers in business markets are able to answer this question. And yet the ability to pinpoint the value of a product or service for one's customers—especially those whose costs are driven by what they purchase—increasingly look to purchasing as a way to increase profits and therefore pressure suppliers to reduce prices. To persuade customers to focus on total costs rather than simply on acquisition price, a supplier must have an understanding of what its customers value, and would value.*[30]

Jean Claude Usunier advocates that price is a critical part of the communications between buyer and seller. In his view, it is impossible to separate human relations from transactions: each party wants to make a good deal. Furthermore, the way they make the deal is significant. For some clients, bargaining is part of the transaction, a ritual that adds to the satisfaction. Bargaining in the Middle East, for example, commences with standard indicators of respect and common interest, with friendliness and fraternity being an important part of the transaction. People of other cultures find bargaining to be distasteful. They prefer to buy a product or service from a recognised outlet at a stated price, with clear conditions for service as part of the transaction.

Apart from the relationship between the client and the seller, Usunier believes price is sometimes used as a tactical weapon. Prices can be manipulated in order to get new market share or to increase client brand loyalty. Objectives that an organisation may pursue include achieving maximum organisation profits, reaching a profit target level, promoting the image of the organisation, eliminating competitors or setting a price at parity with competitors. [31]

Whatever importance your own clients attribute to price, the balanced score-card is put into play when managers define the client-oriented strategy in terms of three goals, these being time, performance and service, and price, and then translate the goals into specific measures. Strategic objectives could include, for example, the delivery of products to the client's door before the expected arrival date, cutting the number of defective products in half, visiting each client's factory at least twice per annum and creating boutique products to meet the needs of particular clients.

The cost of the product to the client must also be measured. The price of the goods themselves is one component of cost. Other costs that a client must incur are ordering costs, delivery costs, stamp duty, handling, inspecting and paying for the goods. One organisation may sell its products for a higher price per unit, but may nonetheless be cheaper than its competitors overall because it can save the client in other ways, such as ordering, delivery charges, supplying products free of defects and lowering the administrative burden of the purchase to the client.

To track the goal of achieving improved delivery times, an organisation can measure the percentage of total sales that are delivered to the client's door outside the time period specified by the goal. In this way, deliveries that fail to meet the goal are reported. Of course, when measuring client service, it is important to align your goals with the expectations of your clients.

World-class organisations are remarkably purposeful in their approaches to providing new value for their clients. The reason should be obvious: *they have to be.* Knowing what the clients value should not be an accident; neither does it come from exclusive reliance on what they tell you. It is derived from a process which treats the clients' business as *your* business.

ALIGNING YOUR GOALS WITH THE EXPECTATIONS OF YOUR CLIENTS

What is the meaning of the goal 'reducing the delivery time to the client'? One client may think that delivery time refers to a ships' ETA, and another may think it is any time within seven days of the ETA. One thing is clear, delivery time must be defined by the clients at some stage, either by a survey (it could be anonymous) or through direct client contact. The result is that you empower employees to use performance measures for goals that reflect the way your performance is viewed through the lenses of your clients.

BENCHMARKING CUSTOMER SATISFACTION

A variant is using internal data to set your customer satisfaction objective. Benchmarking is the search for industry best practices that lead to superior performance. This means that you search right through your industry to find best practices in all of the areas of client concern. What you then do is formulate your goals in line with the best practices. The rationale for doing this is that an organisation with good strategies can adapt to and exploit the particular competitive environment that it confronts.

'Benchmarking', as it is known, can work well where your organisation is similar to the ones you have compared it with, but not so useful when you offer niche products to your clients. Benchmarking for performance measures is considered in detail in Chapter 11.

MEASURING CLIENT COMPLAINTS

Some commentators have suggested that measuring the number of client complaints is not useful in determining client satisfaction. The reason for this, they argue, is that the clients who do not complain represent the 'silent majority'. The fact is, they say, complainers' complaints are usually unrepresentative of the typical client. It is well known that most dissatisfied clients suffer in silence. When clients become completely frustrated, they more often than not walk instead of complain.

If that paradox is recognised, then proactive organisations can solicit feedback by making it easier for clients to complain. While an effective complaint system is a useful tool, it is no substitute for proactive client satisfaction management.

Client satisfaction management has a great deal to do with *listening* to the needs of clients. In the 1950s, Bill Bowerman was an athletics coach at the University of Oregon. Like most other coaches he saw the existing athletic footwear as a serious impediment to improved performance. Unlike others, he did something about it. He experimented with new shoe designs tailored for individual athletes and events. Over time, he developed an approach to design and construction which had a major impact on comfort and performance.

Bowerman, along with Phillip Knight set up Blue Ribbon Sports—which later became known as Nike. By 1985, Nike had grown to a billion-dollar organisation and was a clear market leader in all of the major markets worldwide. From the outset Nike had a major advantage over the competition: it listened. The company's sales team were all runners; they travelled to athletics meetings and talked with the athletes and listened to their problems.

By 1986, Nike lost its market leadership of the American footwear market to Reebok. Reebok had analysed what aerobic fans wanted from their sports shoes at a time when other manufacturers were run by sports jocks who made the sorts of shoes they liked themselves. Nike, having listened so carefully to the needs of athletes and joggers, had failed to do the same for this rapidly emerging market segment. It paid the price.[32]

If clients have views which suggest the relationship between them and the organisation requires improvement, then their views must be sought on how it can be improved. This requires skilful interviewing, asking the client to suggest ideas on how the causes of their dissatisfaction could be dealt with. [33]

The balanced scorecard motivates ideas on how organisations can renew their businesses and re-engineer their systems to meet the changing needs of clients worldwide. Clients are telling you what they want loud and clear. All you have to do is listen to them.

DENTIFYING CLIENT-FOCUSED MEASURES

In identifying measures, remember Price's Dictum 'no measurement without recording, no recording without analysis, no analysis without action'. Any data must form the basis of a decision or action.

Foundations

Measures are required to ensure that desired outcomes are delivered. Implicit in this statement is the concept of performance standards around which are built corrective actions, escalation procedures, improvement plans and the like. These outcomes will be impacted through process control and improvement.

It is important, therefore, that measures are in place not only for things that may go wrong (or have been known to have gone wrong in the past), but also for all things that must go right in order to satisfy clients' requirements. Thus, it is important that any set of measures is reasonably complete and does not simply reflect the things that are easy to measure.

All process effectiveness measures should relate, directly or indirectly, to the client. These measures will be derived from client requirements. Accordingly, before measures can be established, it is vital to know for each major client segment the client's requirements of the process. Client requirements fall into three categories:

▶ basic expectations;
▶ spoken requirements;
▶ delight factors.

All types of requirements should be known.

Over time, these expectations change. There is a distinction between needs, requirements and expectations. A client need is an instance in which a want exists. A need exists independent of any product or service provider; for example, a need might be to clothe oneself for protection against the elements. A requirement is a specification of a component of a product or service offering that would satisfy a need. Client expectations, on the other hand, are about what clients anticipate is likely to happen. They can be influenced by such things as media, advertising, personal needs, past experiences, competition and overseas experience to name a few. What was once a spoken requirement soon becomes a basic expectation. Similarly, clients start requesting delight factors once they know they are possible. Thus, constant monitoring and updating of measures to reflect current client requirements is necessary.

Basic expectations

Unspoken requirements are things clients expect and therefore do not explicitly mention when asked what they want. The exception is when clients complain. Failing to deliver these unspoken requirements is frequently more serious than failing to meet a spoken requirement. For instance, imagine ordering a home-delivered pizza and pasta arrives! Compare how you would feel about this, as opposed to a small pizza arriving instead of the large one you ordered.

It is not altogether easy to quantify basic expectations. Subject to the qualifications set out above, complaints analysis can assist in identifying some of your clients' basic expectations. A useful measure could be the percentage of client complaints to total orders per month.

Spoken requirements

Spoken requirements refer to the things clients say they want. By ordering a large pizza rather than a small one you are stating your requirement as to size. Spoken requirements can be determined through a two-phase market research process.

First, qualitative market research is undertaken. This involves holding focus groups or direct interviews with clients. From these discussions, their needs and requirements are identified. The problem with this method for small businesses is primarily cost. For small businesses, a viable alternative is a suggestion box on the premises. If the business is conducted over the internet, then an email address may be provided. Depending on the level of response from clients, it may then be possible to learn what is important to clients. The measures should follow. This phase is usually sufficient for small firms.

Second, quantitative market research is undertaken. Specific information is gathered from a wider population of clients to determine the relative priority of each of these spoken requirements. From this research, a list of clients' spoken requirements and priorities are collated. While this data is being collected, it is often useful to collect perceptions of performance on these requirements. This data can be collected for competitors' performance as well.

Delight factors

Delight factors are unspoken requirements which, if provided, give the client a pleasant surprise. To draw on the pizza example from above, this could be receiving a complimentary bottle of soft drink with the pizza. What happens to the level of client satisfaction in your organisation when you package your product or service offerings with a 'delight factor'?

Identifying these factors can be difficult. It requires skill in handling the client interviews or focus groups and revolves around being able to 'peel back' the client requirements to fundamental needs. Approaches like 'Why do you want that?', 'How do you use it?', 'What value does it provide, and why?' and 'What could you do to make those outcomes better?' can yield some insight.

CLIENT MEASURES — THE MEASUREMENT PROCESS

Having identified what to measure, you need to know how to do it. Client measures fall into three types: results measures, overview in-process measures and detailed in-process measures. Table 7 contains a number of client measures which may be useful for your organisation. Additional measures are set out in the Appendix.

Results measures look, through the lens of the client, at the extent to which the process has met their requirements. Usually, a performance measure on each key client requirement, both spoken and unspoken, will be defined. Overview in-process measures must always be derived from client requirements. They are internal process performance measures. While results measures are lag performance indicators, overview in-process measures are designed to provide lead indicators of results. Collectively, a well-defined set of overview in-process measures provide a complete view of the end-to-end process performance.

Overview in-process measures can be determined through consideration of each key client requirement—spoken and unspoken. A set of measures can then be

TABLE 7   **Client measures**

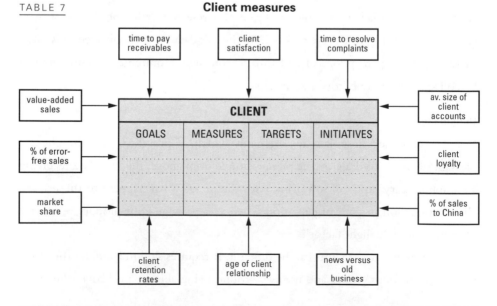

defined which cover every key client requirement. Accordingly, there should be a strong correlation between results and overview in-process measures.

Overview in-process measures should be:

▶ Controllable through process operation or design changes.

▶ Independent of process design concept.

▶ Predictive of client perceptions.

▶ Quantifiable.

Overview in-process measures are either measured independently in the process or are aggregated from other detailed in-process measures.

All detailed in-process measures should relate to at least one client requirement. Detailed in-process measures are used to monitor the performance of individual process steps or operations and can be used at a local level, as an early warning system, to initiate corrective action to reduce variation and improve performance. These measures are used by people operating within the process. Detailed in-process measures can be determined in the following manner:

▶ Agree on the process top-down flowchart.

▶ Agree upon operational definitions for each step: start, finish, inclusions, exclusions, inputs, outputs and outcomes.

▶ Define a valid sampling scheme for each measure.

▶ Identify within each step key tasks that relate to meeting client requirements.

▶ Select and define measures for each of these steps and operations. These measures will assist in determining the capability of an organisation to meet the client requirements.

▶ Agree upon an operational definition for the measure.

Process improvement measures

To undertake any form of process improvement, both results and overview in-process measures are required. These assist in identifying opportunities for improvement and setting priorities.

Where process innovation is necessary to bring about higher client satisfaction rates, detailed in-process measures are not usually necessary for process analysis. However, as the new process is designed, appropriate detailed in-process measures for the new process must be specified.

SUMMARY

World–class organisations have a clear focus on their clients. They understand that it is necessary to measure important areas like 'client satisfaction' and 'client complaint' rates to retain existing clients and to win new ones, so that long-term profits improve. In this chapter you have seen why organisations must focus on their clients and measure the key perspectives of value for them. The readjustment issues faced by organisations once they find that their mission statements are not aligned with clients' expectations were also examined. Of course, to make the chapter complete, there was a comprehensive treatment on measuring client complaints.

What must we excel at from an internal perspective?

Don't ever take a fence down until you know why it was put up. ROBERT FROST

A lot of money that should be cut out of the federal bureaucracies would be found if you had a really serious effort to review operations from a quality perspective. I read in Fortune a great article on General Electric under Jack Welch. When he started this sort of review, they found—and this is a very well run company . . .—they found there were four people working in a room sending copies of reports to 24 different people . . . No one ever read the report. Everybody always thought someone else was. When they cancelled this operation, they saved $150,000 a year. That's the sort of thing I am convinced is out there all over the government.

DEMOCRATIC PRESIDENTIAL NOMINEE GOV. BILL CLINTON, AUGUST 1992

Client-oriented measures are vital. They do not define, however, what organisations must change internally to meet their clients' expectations. Delivering excellent client performance flows directly from an organisation's processes to get its products out to the marketplace. Using the balanced scorecard approach, an organisation sets internal business process objectives, then works towards achieving them (see Table 8). Re-engineering the critical internal processes that enable an organisation to satisfy clients' needs requires breakthrough thinking. This chapter considers how an organisation can maximise the value of the balanced scorecard by managing and re-engineering its processes. Effective process management and process re-engineering efforts depend on supervisors who possess appropriate project management skills. This chapter examines the minimum project management skills that are required for that purpose.

Your internal business process measures (e.g. productivity, safety, employee skills, quality and cycle time) have a significant but often understated influence on your clients' levels of satisfaction. Goals and targets must be set, and improvement initiatives implemented. Chapter 9, Designing Your Balanced Scorecard, covers these issues in greater detail. If sales are not as high as you would like (because client satisfaction rates are too low), then by measuring the performance of the internal processes of the organisation, you can identify processes functioning inefficiently. The next step is to manage these processes. If process management does not lift sales, then on the basis of the criteria set out later in this chapter, the process must be either eliminated or re-engineered.

You can maximise your gains in this area by complementing the re-engineered internal processes with a tailored information management system. Possessing a good internal costing structure and information system is vital. To make people in the

TABLE 8 **Internal business process dimension**

Balanced Scorecard
DIMENSIONS AND OBJECTIVES

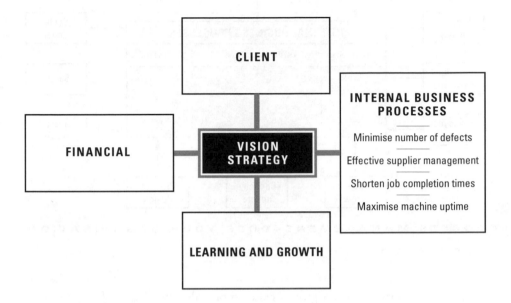

organisation aware of problems (e.g. a blow out in cycle time), a responsive information reporting system is required. If the information reporting system is functionally obsolete (i.e. unreflective of the activities undertaken by the organisation, or commercially unresponsive such that maintenance is required constantly), then the organisation risks losing its competitive advantage because problems cannot be remedied quickly. A tardy response to process problems can put a dent in profits. In one South African manufacturing organisation, Daughters of Sanwa, the balanced scorecard report is released just days after balance date each month. The organisation has no need at present to upgrade its information reporting system.

One Australian car insurance organisation has implemented the balanced scorecard producing clear results from the process. Process design, control and improvement have yielded significant improvements across the organisation. Through the claims process improvement program, several instances of unnecessary checking were discovered causing one process to take anything up to twelve weeks to complete. Now through process improvements implemented by key staff the turnaround time on that process is approximately 48 hours. See Table 9 for often used process measures. Additional measures are set out in the Appendix.

TABLE 9

Internal business process measures

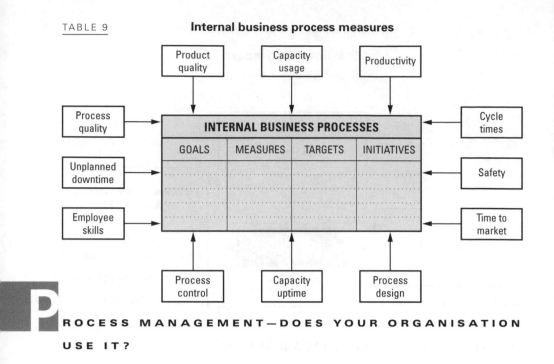

PROCESS MANAGEMENT—DOES YOUR ORGANISATION USE IT?

Every business process or sub-process exists to provide a needed product or service for a defined client. These products and services are produced within the process according to defined requirements, rules or constraints. The process requires materials and information which are provided by suppliers, clients and the resources allocated to the process.

Vertical organisation structures once served the needs of Australian organisations well. Not anymore. The arranging of work into like functions was suited to the needs of an uneducated workforce. It simplified employee supervision and training, maximised managerial control and had little dependence on the free flow of data.

However, a new model is needed for world-class organisations. Work can be organised and managed as an end-to-end process, rather than as the sum of disjointed functions. Once the concept of process management is firmly rooted in the organisation, it becomes possible to see real and lasting improvements in process performance. The balanced scorecard tracks these improvements by measuring key indicators of performance. (See the Appendix for a comprehensive list of internal business process performance measures.) Outside a process management framework, process re-engineering efforts have little chance of lasting success.

Process management requires an integrated approach to the management of an end-to-end process, including its lower-level activities, which produces a product or service for a given client. This concept goes beyond organisation structures. It encompasses everything necessary to identify, produce and deliver a quality product or service to a fully satisfied client. When an organisation chooses to manage the processes, the organisation's structure and rules are no longer the focus of its efforts. The total satisfaction of the client becomes the reason for the organisation to exist. Performance is now measured by how well the product or service is received by the client, not how well one activity within the process is performed. The balanced scorecard captures this vital information.

Another aspect of this management philosophy relates to the idea of *managing the mission* compared with managing the organisation. Simply stated, if the process directly supports the mission of the organisation, then by managing the process you are, in turn, managing the mission. Many organisations spend too much time managing the rules of the organisation. They give little attention to the process by which the mission is being accomplished or the products and services being produced. By incorporating the philosophy of process management, the vision becomes the emphasis as opposed to whether or not the organisation is being managed.

The process management model

The culmination of the evolution of the process is the Process Management Model. Notice Table 10 shows the five parts of the model: (1) the mission; (2) the client; (3) the product; (4) the process; and (5) an information architecture. The concept is simple. If an organisation does not have clients, then it does not have a product. If it does not have a product, it will not need a process to produce the product. If it

TABLE 10   **Process management model**

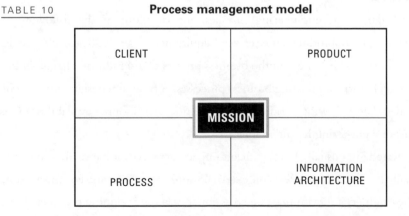

does not have the need for the process, eliminate it. Of course, this is all taken in the context of the mission of the organisation.

LEVELS OF PROCESS IMPROVEMENT

Another way to look at a business process is as a group of interrelated tasks and activities that accomplish a defined goal or mission of an organisation. By this definition, even the largest organisations have no more than five or six core business processes. It is the improvement of these processes on a continuous basis—and their measurement—that allows organisations to be able to continue to perform their mission during a time of dwindling resources. Let us look at three aspects of process improvement:

1.   New process design
2.   Process redesign (re-engineering)
3.   Continuous process improvement

New process design

New process design is performed based on a change of mission or strategic plan. This can occur during the design and implementation stages of your balanced scorecard. New process design would be required if a previously outsourced function was brought inhouse. The distinguishing characteristic of new process design is that there is no baseline from which to work. Benchmarking can be critical to the success of a new process design effort. Benchmarking is covered in Chapter 11.

Process redesign

Process redesign (or re-engineering) implies one or more of the following: a significant change in product and service requirements, a significant change in controls or constraints imposed on the business process or a significant change in the technological platform supporting business processes. A process redesign effort might also be undertaken following a radical change in financial resource availabilities (i.e. budget cuts or right-sizing requirements).

Process redesign usually has significant impacts across organisational boundaries and generally has impacts or effects on external suppliers and clients. For this reason, a process re-engineering team must be cross-functional, by including members from all impacted divisions. Process redesign can have impacts on the organisational structures supporting the business process. This means that re-engineering teams must have the support and backing of senior leaders if improvement initiatives are to be given frank consideration by review and approval personnel. How can processes be redesigned?

Step 1.   The first step is to identify your business processes by going directly to your mission statement and strategic plan. The need for each business process in your organisation should be based on these documents.

Step 2.   Next, identify your clients and suppliers. Your clients determine what products and services your processes should provide. Your suppliers provide the raw materials and components your process will use in building your products and services.

Step 3.   Then you analyse all of the activities that take place in your process that are in the value-chain between what you get from your suppliers and what you deliver to your clients. Those activities that add value to your products and services should be strengthened and optimised. All other activities should be reduced or eliminated. A more detailed look at the step-by-step methodology that you use to do this is set out below.

Process improvement

Continuous process improvement embodies the philosophy that no matter how good something is, it can be improved. And if you do not improve it, someone else will, who may steal all of your clients.

Process improvement actions are defined as those improvements which you can undertake with minimal impact on external suppliers, clients and other organisations within the functional area. The focus of this level of process improvement is an emphasis on reducing the overhead associated with self-imposed controls and restrictions, eliminating non-value-added activities, reducing non-value-added costs, optimising available resources with respect to process and activity output requirements, and other improvements that can be made within the authority level of the target organisational element.

BUSINESS PROCESS RE-ENGINEERING—A TOOL FOR CHANGE

You may have heard a great deal about business process re-engineering through business journals and trade publications, published books or in training workshops. Business process re-engineering seems like the hottest management trend to hit the business and governmental communities. It is more than a fad, and can bring a new emphasis on creativity.

Re-engineering is definitely not the same as 'reorganising' or 'downsizing'. Business process re-engineering looks at what work is required to be done, not how the organisation is structured. Until the processes are designed for an organisation to produce products and services for its clients, organisation structures are not defined. An organisation's structure is then designed to best support that process.

Re-engineering is not simply about making an organisation more efficient. You can have the most efficient organisation in the industry, but unless it effectively serves its clients, it is still of no value. Re-engineering creates flexible delivery of client-value solutions. In this context, client value refers to lower cost, higher quality, or shorter response time. In implementing quality, most organisations forget the No. 1 principle in quality theory, which says the client defines the quality. In turn, when one of your clients says quality, do they mean product or service quality? Or is it relationship quality? Do they mean credit quality? Do they mean performance or conformance of features or design, or do they mean packaging?

You can use the balanced scorecard to derive the most benefits from process re-engineering. Business process re-engineering has four objectives. By achieving these objectives you can assist the organisation to realise its vision by:

1. **Reducing the cost of doing business**. In today's environment, cost reductions play an increasingly important role. Business process re-engineering aims to reduce the cost of business by eliminating from organisations their:
    — inefficient processes;
    — inefficient review and approval cycles;
    — obsolete policies and controls;
    — wasteful management overhead.

2. **Encouraging a fee-for-service**. If your products and services have value, then your clients *should be willing and able to pay for them*. Your internal business process goals, therefore, need to relate to the application of more businesslike practices. By determining client requirements and then meeting those client requirements competitively, you can provide more client value at a lower cost than before. Increasingly, your clients, who may be captive now, will have (if they do not already) other suppliers and service providers to obtain what they need to perform their job, just as you can switch from your present suppliers.

3. **Promoting continuous process improvement**. Process improvement is not a single undertaking. Responding to clients' needs, using quality inputs and making processes more efficient and effective by insisting on more innovative resources management is a continuous process. Even if you have fundamentally redesigned a major business process, it does not mean that you can halt the continuous improvement process. Business process re-engineering, coupled with a program of continuous improvements (discussed in Chapter 5, How Can We Continue to Add Value?) can put an organisation in an advantageous position when the time for budget justification arrives.

4. **Instilling confidence in leadership**. Line managers are accountable for outcomes and exercise discretion with respect to business process re-engineering. Leadership is critical to the success of any performance re-engineering effort.

Business process re-engineering techniques

Alignment of the operation of your processes to your strategic objectives will improve your ability to monitor organisational progress. Process re-engineering can involve a variety of techniques. Some or all of the techniques shown below may be relevant for your organisation. A decision as to which technique(s) to employ should be based as much on organisational size, competitive pressures and affordability as on the expected benefits you expect to derive.

▶   **Activity modelling**. Activity modelling assists you with understanding how your processes really work. You use activity modelling to describe how processes function, and how you want them to function, based on your redesign criteria. To transform your processes, you decompose a business process step-by-step into activities (i.e. sub-processes) that make up the process. This results in a multi-level diagram that corresponds to the way you do work. Each activity is shown in a diagram, complete with the inputs to that activity, the outputs of that activity, the controls or constraints on the way you perform the activity and the mechanisms or factors of production consumed by the activity in transforming inputs to outputs.

▶ **Data modelling**. Information can link together independent parts of an organisation. Data modelling is a technique for accurately describing exactly what information you need to do every activity that makes up the internal process you perform. A data model shows, in relation to all of the objects which an organisation values enough to keep data about, the attributes of each object, and the relationships between and among objects. One of the results of data modelling is a clear delineation of business rules which are statements that constrain the way your functions and their processes work. The level at which you will be called upon to do data modelling is easily learned, even if you are not technically inclined. If you can write a functional procedure or design a simple form, you can successfully model data with the assistance of a facilitator.

▶ **Activity-based costing**. This technique allows you to determine the costs of producing your primary products and services. ABC is an extension of activity modelling and, while it requires a great deal of work to produce the numbers, it too is an easily learned technique. There are a great number of software packages available on the market which can perform ABC automated costing.

▶ **Economic analysis**. Applying the principles of business process re-engineering to your organisation's business processes can result in a slate of improvement opportunities. There will always be alternative means of implementing process improvements. Economic analysis gives you the capability to determine the costs and benefits associated with alternative investment opportunities, taking into account the life cycle characteristics of each investment. Economic analysis also presents the decision data in equally valued dollars (taking the time value of money into consideration), as well as the risks associated with making decisions about future conditions and performance.

▶ **Best business practices**. Most line managers ask two questions about their accountability areas:

— Is this the best way to do it?

— How does what I do compare with what others do who have the same responsibilities?

The first question can be answered by using best practice techniques; the second question by using benchmarking techniques. These techniques are discussed in more detail in Chapter 10, Implementing Your Balanced Scorecard. For now, you should get a general sense of what is available to assist you in your endeavour to improve the business processes.

Business process re-engineering methodology

Below are six steps to follow when re-engineering internal business processes.

1. Define

Define functional objectives; determine the functional management strategy to be followed in streamlining and standardising processes; and establish the process, data and information systems baselines from which to begin process improvement. A framework is established by defining these baselines, objectives and strategies for the function.

2. Analyse

Analyse the business processes to eliminate non-value-added processes, simplify and streamline limited value added processes, and examine all processes to identify more effective and efficient alternatives to the process, data and system baselines.

3. Evaluate

Evaluate alternatives to baseline processes through a preliminary functional economic analysis to select a preferred course of action.

4. Plan

Plan implementation of the preferred course of action by developing detailed statements of requirements, baseline impacts, costs, benefits and schedules.

5. Approve

Extract from the planning data the information needed to finalise the functional economic analysis, which is used by senior management to approve the proposed process improvements and any associated data or system changes.

6. Execute

Execute the approved process and data changes, and provide functional management oversight of any associated information system changes.

USING PROJECT MANAGEMENT

Successful business process management and re-engineering programs depend on supervisors having adequate project management skills. Project management is the process of defining a project's requirements, planning the tasks and ensuring the project is implemented so that it is completed to the performance specification, on time and to cost, to the client's requirements. In essence, each task during your working day can be considered a project. Project management is a top-down approach beginning with the development of senior managers/supervisors. They will, in turn, develop, manage, coach and mentor their staff.

SUMMARY

The balanced scorecard should be based on the key internal business processes required to realise a strategy. An organisation's key processes are those activities which create client value and which provide the organisation with a competitive advantage. If the processes are not currently supporting the strategy, then a process management or process re-engineering effort may be required. The success of the business process re-engineering program is based, in part, on the preparation and readiness of each organisation. Then the business processes should act as vehicles to deliver the capabilities to provide client value.

How can we continue to add value?

Innovation and learning measures
Employee measures
Information technology measures

We will either find a way or make one. HANNIBAL

Does your organisation outstrip the competition as a successful innovator or does it lag behind? By and large there is no more reliable early warning of an organisation's imminent decline than a sharp and persistent drop in its standing as a successful innovator. Equally dangerous is a deterioration in innovative lead time. An organisation's balanced scorecard should show innovative action.[34] Innovation and learning measures evaluate the organisation's skill levels and capacity to consistently deliver quality results. This area recognises that without the right people with the right skills using the right methodologies, business performance can suffer. An organisation's learning and growth objectives support the objectives in the other three areas: client, internal business process and financial.

There are three broad groups of learning and growth measures (also known as continuous improvement measures) with which an organisation should be concerned:

1. innovation and learning measures;
2. employee measures; and
3. information technology measures.

INNOVATION AND LEARNING MEASURES

Innovation and learning utilises measures that track ideas and inventiveness capable of producing radical improvements in the existing organisation, or even a new organisation. You can measure innovation and learning by monitoring the key drivers which appear in Table 11. Additional innovation measures are set out in the Appendix.

A manufacturing organisation may be aiming to reconfigure its product offerings to client demands. This could involve decreasing the production of products for which the organisation expects demand to fall and increasing the production of those products whose demand is tipped to rise. A manufacturing improvement goal is forward looking—it directs management to consider the future product mix of the organisation. A 'ten-four' program could be used. That is where, say, the defect rate is decreased by a factor of ten over four years. When continuous improvement goals utilise the right measures, they can have an enormously positive impact on staff productivity levels.

In order to achieve this large-step improvement and pursue this extra

TABLE 11

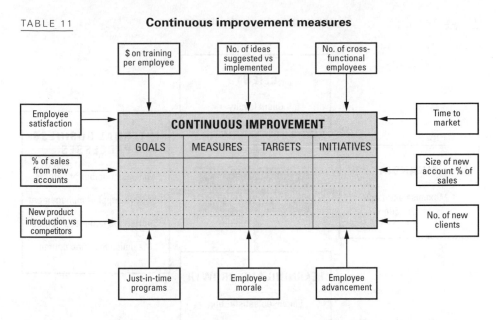

Continuous improvement measures

dimension in quality, one Australian motor car insurer has added two new tools to its tool kit: re-engineering and benchmarking.

EMPLOYEE MEASURES

The people are the key to the success of an organisation. An often quoted cannon is 'a happy worker is the most productive worker'. Suppose that one of an organisation's client objectives is to improve client satisfaction levels. If, for a particular reporting period, the satisfaction rate is below acceptable parameters, then by monitoring employee performance at the same time, it is possible to identify if (and to what extent) low employee morale is a major cause of the poor client satisfaction rate. This is reflected in Table 12.

Accordingly, measures of employee performance should be used to answer the following questions:

▶ Do we have the right skills and qualified staff to ensure quality results?

▶ Are we tracking the development of new skills important to our business/ mission needs?

▶ Are we using recognised approaches and methodologies for building and managing our projects?

TABLE 12

Learning and growth dimension

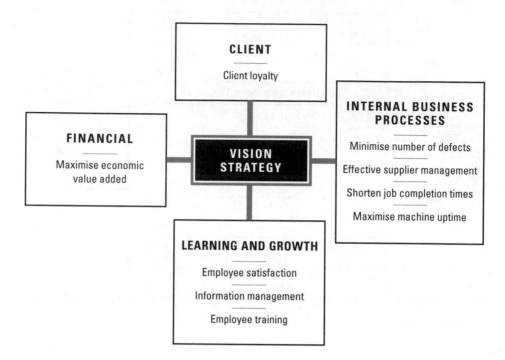

▶ Are we providng our staff with the proper tools, training and incentives to perform their tasks?

To answer these questions, an organisation must measure workforce competency and development, advanced technology use, methodology currency and employee satisfaction and retention.

Workforce competency and development

The best way to measure workforce competency and development in an organisation or a plant is to measure directly the percentage of staff trained in the use of new technologies and techniques. Ideally, this should include everybody in the plant: the direct production people, the sales people, the engineers, the administrative people and the managers. Often it is not possible to do this because 'indirect' people may work on products related to more than one plant, or they may be located in another facility and it is difficult to assign them to a specific product range.

Correspondingly, a complementary measure is the percentage of staff professionally certified. Take the case of a law firm. Is the percentage of legally qualified staff going up or down? Is there a positive relationship between this measure and client satisfaction rates? Clearly, in order to support the achievement of the internal business process objectives, an organisation needs to ensure that a particular standard of workforce competency and development is maintained and improved upon over time.

Advanced technology use

Many people are not familiar with the use of computer applications. Advanced technology use can shorten the time it takes for a staff member to complete a task, the results are more likely to be correct (because of checks and balances in place within the software package), an audit trail exists and the knowledge of how to perform a task is no longer 'in someone's head'. More generally, it is critical for staff to improve their technology skills because high-tech, technological applications are here to stay.

Accordingly, the measure of the percentage of employees skilled in advanced technology applications can potentially explain why an organisation is or is not meeting its set internal business process objectives. For example, AS Tools (an Australian tool-making small business) has typically made die casts by hand. The processes involved are very labour intensive. Whilst the material costs are high, the overall price a client must pay for a job are substantially comprised of labour costs. When AS Tools implemented its balanced scorecard, one of its internal business process objectives was to achieve a 20% improvement in job completion times. What happened though, was a massive blow-out in job turnaround times. The reason was because other industry participants were turning to computer-based tool making methodologies which were cheaper and quicker. With its accountant, AS Tools measured the percentage of its employees skilled in advanced technology use. Four employees had the skills. AS Tools purchased new plant and equipment, and utilised those employees' skills and is now on the road to reducing its job completion times.

Methodology currency

What is the currency of the application methods in use? Is the organisation practising methods which were used 20 years ago and which have been superseded in other organisations?

Workplace flexibility is concerned with an organisation's ability to make today what the client wants today, and to change effectively as client needs change. Traditional organisations meet clients' needs by maintaining their stock levels. World-class organisations build flexibility into their internal business processes so they can make-to-order in often short lead times.

Accordingly, flexibility measures are measures of an organisation's ability to meet client demands. Flexibility can be measured by the level of cross-functional training, the cycle time from placing an order to shipping the goods, the degree of commonality of component parts throughout the products, the degree of common processes across the production floor, the adaptability of the product design and the position of variability within the products.[35]

Employee satisfaction and retention

World-class organisations understand that their people are their most important asset. Issues such as morale, trust, teamwork and leadership are important considerations. Employee morale and teamwork can be ascertained using measures of employee turnover and number of business days lost due to absenteeism. Morale can also be gauged from measures that monitor the level of employee participation, such as the percentage of employees on participation teams. The applicability of this measure to an organisation will depend very much on the culture of the organisation, and whether the culture promotes teamwork or individualism. Even the number of suggestions per employee, the percentage of suggestions implemented, the percentage of employees currently in training and the average number of certified skills per person are good measures.

World-class organisations measure leadership using personnel surveys and work environment measures. Depending on an organisation's requirements, a highly sophisticated measure can be developed. A simple anonymous survey will suffice for many organisations, which asks questions such as 'Does your supervisor make you feel part of a team'?

NFORMATION TECHNOLOGY MEASURES

From small businesses to large multinationals, organisations are relying increasingly on information technology. IT measures, like employee measures, complement the client, internal business process and financial measures. Broadly, there are four IT issues of which organisations should be aware:

1. strategic information management;
2. IT investment and procurement;
3. business process analysis; and
4. data and network management.

Statregic information management

To meet increasing demands, managers must keep pace with evolving management practices and skills needed to define critical information needs and to select, apply and control changing information technologies. However, while leaders have emerged in all industries, in the public sector few organisations have learned how to strategically manage information and information technology to achieve effective results.

To identify opportunities that will enhance the capability of management teams to manage information and technology, an organisation can monitor the number of self-assessments every year. Ideally, all staff should take part in these asssessments.

IT investment and procurement

IT investment and procurement metrics answer the question: how can we improve our ability to make cost-effective IT investment decisions that support our mission-related goals? IT investment is often one of the most expensive investments an organisation can make. In recent years, organisations with older IT systems will have invested money to make the system year 2000 compliant, or alternatively, bought a new package off the shelf. Off-the-shelf packages often suffer high failure rates and can offer limited benefits. As a result, organisations have not been able to take full advantage of the opportunties that key information technologies offer, such as inter-departmental information sharing and electronic delivery of benefits.

Useful measures in this area should identify ways to improve organisational control and accountability for the money spent on IT investments, and identify ways to maximise return and minimise risks in IT expenditure and investment. They should assist organisations with taking early corrective action to reduce the risks of their IT acquisitions costing substantially more than estimated, taking much longer to get up and running than planned or being unsuccessful in lowering costs, improving productivity or enhancing program service delivery.

Business process analysis

How can your organisation effectively use information and IT to reduce costs and increase service levels to the clients? All organisations are faced with rising client expectations and severe resource limitations, but must produce an environment in which the effectiveness of the organisation's decision making and service delivery depends directly on their ability to take advantage of IT. To obtain the greatest advantage of IT, organisations must analyse and modernise the business processes that support their mission-related objectives before acquiring technology.

Data and network management

Organisations are increasingly relying on information technology to store, process and transmit information that is critical to their operations. Is your organisation effectively and efficiently ensuring the availability, integrity and confidentiality of information resources critical to your operations?

Securing this information to ensure appropriate levels of integrity, confidentiality and availability is essential. In addition, organisations must learn to efficiently manage growing volumes of data and the increasingly complex support systems used to process and access this data. However, many organisations are in the early stages of learning to efficiently manage these information resources and identify, evaluate and address the associated risks. The process begins by implementing appropriate measures.

Useful measures here include the percentage of staff who have 'global' access to all files over the network, frequency of login and email password changes, as well as the percentage of network downtime or interruption.

SUMMARY

Continuous improvement, change, flexibility and responsiveness are essential to an organisation's learning and growth. Innovation is about finding new ways of delivering client value. In order to remain successful, a world-class organisation needs to reinvent value, and determine new methodologies to produce positive results on an ongoing basis. They need to craft new internal relationships to stay ahead of their competitors. No organisation can achieve and maintain world-class status without continually evaluating and re-evaluating its situation for new opportunities with a clear focus on employee and IT measures.[36]

How do we look to our shareholders?

Financial benchmarks for comparison

Common size measures

Liquidity measures

Efficiency measures

Solvency measures

Profitability measures

How to use economic value added as a management tool

Don't think there are no crocodiles because the water is calm. MALAYAN PROVERB

Put the shareholder first. That is what organisations which are managing themselves in ways to create and increase shareholder wealth are doing. How organisations rate in terms of their ability to contribute to shareholder value can depend on how an organisation defines and measures success.

Among the financial evaluation tools are sales, profits, return on shareholders' equity, return on assets and return on net assets. Even though the balanced scorecard complements traditional financial measures with softer, non-financial measures, the financial measures are still important for the success of an organisation. Accordingly, it is important to develop financial objectives, goals, targets and measures for this dimension as shown in Table 13.

This chapter examines five principal types of measures. These measures can track the financial drivers to determine whether an organisation is achieving its financial objectives or not. They are: common size measures, liquidity measures, efficiency measures, and solvency and profitability measures. Economic value added is a new methodology which may also form part of your measuring tool kit.

TABLE 13 **Financial dimension**

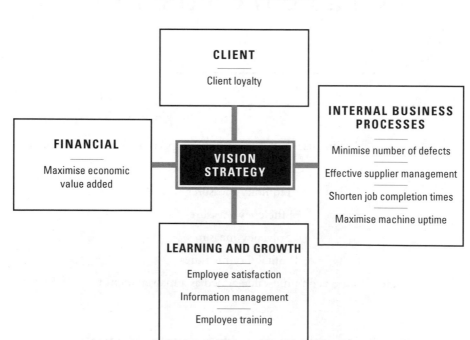

Balanced Scorecard
DIMENSIONS AND OBJECTIVES

CLIENT

Client loyalty

INTERNAL BUSINESS PROCESSES

Minimise number of defects

Effective supplier management

Shorten job completion times

Maximise machine uptime

FINANCIAL

Maximise economic value added

VISION STRATEGY

LEARNING AND GROWTH

Employee satisfaction

Information management

Employee training

Without capital from your shareholders, you would not be in business. Accordingly, it makes sense to measure your performance in a way that is meaningful to shareholders. Typical financial measures would include the ones set out in Table 14.

FINANCIAL BENCHMARKS FOR COMPARISON

Is the current net assets to sales measure good or bad? Is it low enough? Is it too high? You do not want to have too little in the way of current assets, or you may have a liquidity crisis. If you have too much in current assets this implies that you are passing up profitable long-term investment opportunities. There is no one-size-fits-all for financial measures. You must assess the appropriateness of the measures you employ on the basis of some benchmark or basis for comparison.

There are three main benchmarks. The first is the organisation's history. You always want to review the measures for the organisation this year to what they were in previous years. This enables you to discover favourable or unfavourable trends that are developing gradually over time, as well as spikes and troughs that have changed sharply in the space of time of just one year.

The second benchmark is to compare the organisation with specific competitors. If your competitors are public companies on the Australian Stock Exchange, then you can obtain copies of their annual financial reports and compare each of your measures

TABLE 14 **Financial measures**

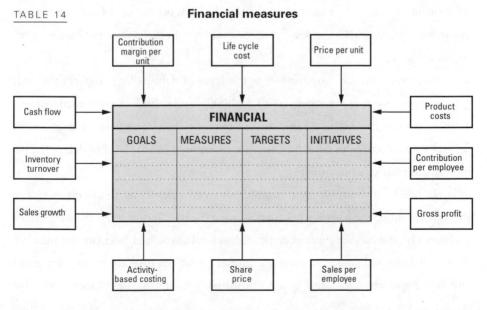

with each of theirs. This approach is developed more in Chapter 11, Benchmarking Your Performance Measures. By finding where your measures differ, you may determine what you are doing better or worse than the competition.

The third benchmark is industry-wide comparison. A number of organisations gather industry-wide information and publish the results, such as Dun and Bradstreet. For example, suppose your current measure of debtors to current assets is 25%, and the industry average is 12%, is that a material difference? Your level of debtors are twice as high as the industry average. This might be a cause for some concern. As a minimum, you should investigate why your measure is particularly high, compared with your industry.

COMMON SIZE MEASURES

Common size measures are an integral tool for small business to conduct financial statement analysis. Suppose that you compared your small business with another. You look to your receivables and see that they are $22,000, while another small business has receivables of $8,000. Does this mean you have poor credit collection processes? Slow paying clients? Before asking questions such as these, you need to clarify how the two businesses are similar, and more importantly, how they differ. Are you twice the size as the other small business? Does the other organisation sell its receivables to a factoring company? The level of receivables depends on the size of your operations compared with theirs. Comparing your receivables with theirs does not create a very useful measure.

However, you can 'common-size' the level of debtors by comparing it with total current assets. If your debtors of $22,000 is one-third of your total current assets and their debtors of $8,000 is one-third of their total current assets, then relative to asset size, both small businesses are keeping a similar level of debtors. This information has value in utility.

To find your common size measures, you need a clear basis for comparison. For the balance sheet, the basis is total assets or total equity. You calculate the measure of each asset on the balance sheet as compared to total assets. You calculate the measure of each liability and equity account as compared with the total equity. For the profit and loss statement, all numbers are compared with gross sales. Once you have calculated the common size measures you can use them to compare your organisation with itself over time, with competitors, and even with industry-wide statistics.

LIQUIDITY MEASURES

Liquidity measures examine whether an organisation is maintaining an appropriate level of liquidity. Too little liquidity can lead to default on loans then bankruptcy. Too much liquidity implies that long-term investments with greater profitability have been missed. The organisation must ensure that it maintains enough, but not too much, liquidity.

The quick measure emphasises an organisation's short-term viability—its ability to stay in business. It compares current assets quickly convertible into cash with current liabilities on the basis that notwithstanding not all current assets are convertible to cash in the very near term, most current liabilities have to be paid in the very near term. For example, inventory, while saleable, takes time to sell. The quick measure compares an organisation's cash, short-term investments and accounts receivable with its current liabilities. Accounts receivable terms can vary from seven days up to 180 days. Accounts receivable are 'quick' assets because factoring companies can convert your receivables into cash almost immediately.

The quick measure is typically used as a measure of *risk*. You should exercise caution when using this measure. No single measure can tell the entire story of an organisation. Measures should be used *cumulatively*. Any one measure can point in the wrong direction.

For example, suppose a company has large balances in cash and short-term investments, and its quick measure might be three. This measure leads you to believe that there is low risk. However, what if the company is losing money at a rapid rate, and the only reason delaying bankruptcy was the sale of a major plant or investment? The sale generated enough cash to meet immediate needs and left an excess, resulting in the high quick measure. How long will this excess last? If the cash and investments are large relative to current liabilities, but small relative to operating costs or long-term liabilities, then liquidity may still be extremely risky.

An organisation seeks to maximise its profits for any given level of risk. This requires the organisation to operate efficiently. A number of measures exist that can help an organisation to assess how efficiently it is operating and allow for comparison between organisations over time. The principal efficiency measures look at the efficient handling of receivables and inventory.

Receivables measures

Ensuring the timely collection of receivables is a universal problem. Once receivables are collected, the money received can be used to retire debt or it can be invested. Upon receipt of the money, you can either pay less interest on debt, or earn more interest. Either way, prompt collection of receivables is desirable.

The receivables turnover measure is a common indicator of efficiency in collecting receivables. It measures how many times during the year your receivables are generated and then collected. To measure the turnover of receivables, you compare your sales on credit with your average accounts receivable balance. The average of accounts receivables is the balance in accounts receivable at the beginning and the end of the year divided by two.

You could compare your level of receivables turnover with that of competitors or your own organisation, but in prior years. However, receivables can be described in terms of how long it takes from point of sale to collection. A useful tool is to convert your receivables turnover into the average age of receivables statistic. This statistic is the outcome of dividing the 365 days in a year by the receivables turnover measure.

Average age of receivables is easier to relate to. Consider whether 68 days is a reasonable average length of time to wait for collection of receivables. If the industry average is 23 days you might be concerned. However, like the quick measure, you want the turnover of receivables or the average age to be neither too low nor too high. If this is important to the shareholders, you might want to make the collection of receivables a strategic objective of the organisation, particularly given the debt interest savings you can realise on receipt of payment.

Inventory measures

The inventory turnover measure is the cost of goods sold divided by the average inventory (beginning plus ending inventory divided by two). If inventory is kept on hand for too long, money is wasted through lost sales revenue that could have been earned, or from interest paid on money borrowed to maintain the inventory. Excessively large inventories can result in excessive warehousing costs, property taxes and product obsolescence. On the other hand, if inventory levels are too low, then sales may be lost.

Industry-wide statistics are usually available for total inventory turnover. In particular, it may be useful to compare the turnover and/or age of inventory separately for raw materials, work in process, and finished goods for manufacturing organisations. For example, a common response to why inventory turnover is slow is that the business is seasonal and the organisation must stockpile finished goods for the busy season, often Christmas. On the other hand, if you examine the inventory measures on a more detailed basis, you may find it is in fact raw materials that are being held for excessive periods of time.

SOLVENCY MEASURES

Liquidity measures are vital for informing an organisation of its ability to meet its obligations in the very near future, but solvency measures take a longer-term view. Solvency measures determine if the organisation has over-extended itself through the use of financial leverage.

Two common solvency measures are the interest coverage measure and the debt-to-equity measure. The former focuses on the ability to meet debt interest payments whilst the latter looks at risk of default. If a bankruptcy does occur, creditors can share in an organisation's assets before the ordinary shareholders can claim any of their equity. The more equity that the owners have in the firm, the greater the likelihood that the organisation's assets will be great enough to protect the claim of all the creditors.

The interest coverage measure compares funds available to pay interest with the total amount of interest that has to be paid. The funds available for interest are an organisation's profits before interest and taxes. As long as the profit before interest and taxes (the operating income) is greater than the amount of interest, an organisation will have enough money to pay the interest owed. The higher this measure is, the more comfortable creditors feel.

Again, you can maintain this measure at a certain level. The appropriate level depends on what is customary in your industry, combined with whether you desire to be more or less highly leveraged than your competitors. The same point holds true for the debt-to-equity measure. There are several different debt-to-equity measures. For example, you can compare long-term debt with shareholders' equity, or total liabilities with shareholders' equity. One common form of the debt-to-equity measure compares an organisation's total liabilities with its total equities (both liabilities and shareholders' equity). The greater the liabilities relative to the total equity, the more risky the organisation.

Alternative measures can be created. Debt-equity is sometimes used to refer to short-term debt compared with shareholders' equity. Debt-equity can focus on how much debt the short-term creditors have invested in the organisation compared with the owners. Another approach is to compare the total current liabilities with the shareholders' equity. None of these measures is clearly superior in value to the others; different industries tend to focus on one or the other as a standard industry practice for consistent comparison purposes.

PROFITABILITY MEASURES

How well did the organisation do? Was the shareholders' wealth improved by the actions the organisation undertook during the year? Profitability measures attempt to show how well the organisation performed, given the level of risk and types of risk it actually assumed during the year. Net income is not a satisfactory measure of profitability because it is a single number without an adequate benchmark.

Return on investment falls into a broad category of profitability measures. There are many definitions for return on investment and this makes it difficult to perform inter-organisation comparisons.

The success of Bausch & Lomb is linked to three strategies: making shareholder interests a high priority, commitment to decentralisation and 'entrepreneurial spirit' and business focus.[37] Kodak relies on return on net assets as the company yardstick. Future goals of the company, its financial performance, wages and dividends will all be measured by this measure. PepsiCo has implemented a shareholder value program which advocates the ownership of share options for employees as a lever to drive superior employee performance. Xerox, like Kodak, believes in the return on assets measure, but recognises that choosing any single measure will not provide a complete picture of the performance of the company.

The problem with using net income solely as a measure of performance is that it ignores the cost of capital used to generate that income. Return on assets evaluates an organisation's return relative to the asset base used to generate the income. That is probably not what the organisation's owners want to know. They seek to know the organisation's earning performance compared with the shareholders' equity. This is commonly called the return on equity or the return on net assets.

Return on assets can be useful for evaluating managers, but inadequate for evaluating the organisation. Return on equity is good for evaluating overall organisation performance, but not for manager evaluation. Most managers do not control an organisation's money; instead they try to use the funds under their authority most efficiently.

Return on equity is a useful measure of the income that an organisation was able to generate relative to the amount of owners' investment in it. Return on equity includes the effect caused by the organisation's degree of leverage. To remove the impact of leverage from your evaluation, you should use return on assets.

Delevered net income means recalculating the organisation's income by assuming that it had no interest expense at all. In doing this, you can put organisations with different decisions regarding the use of borrowed money versus owner-contributed funds all on a comparable basis. You can see how profitable your organisation is relative to the assets it used. You have completely separated any profitability (or loss) created by having used borrowed money instead of owner-invested capital. The way you delever net income is to take the organisation's operating margin (income before interest and tax) and calculate tax directly on that amount, ignoring interest. The result is a net income based on the assumption that there had been no interest expense.

Beware, because not all organisations calculate return on assets in exactly the same way. Some organisations use assets net of depreciation as the basis for comparison. This is how the assets appear on the balance sheet. Some organisations ignore depreciation and use gross assets as a base. The reason for this is to avoid causing an organisation or division to appear to have a very high return on assets simply because its assets are very old and fully depreciated. Such fully depreciated assets cause the base of the measure to be very low and therefore the resulting measure to be very large.

Along the same lines, some organisations use replacement cost instead of historical cost to place divisions in an equal position.

Despite any of these adjustments, use of any of the return on assets measures for evaluation of managers creates undesired incentives. Suppose the organisation and its owners are happy to accept any project with an after-tax rate of return of 7%. One division of the organisation currently has a return on assets of 21%, and a proposed project that would have a 14% return on assets is being evaluated. The manager of the division wants to reject the project entirely if he or she is evaluated based on return on assets. The 14% project, even though profitable, will reduce that division's weighted average return on assets, which is currently 21%. Even though the project is good for the organisation and its owners, it would hurt the manager's performance evaluation.

It is on this basis that many academics recommend the residual income measure. Under this approach, the organisation specifies a minimum required rate of return on its assets. For each project being evaluated, you would multiply the amount of asset investment required for the project by the required rate of return on assets. The result would be subtracted from the profits anticipated from the project. If the project is expected to earn more than the proposed investment multiplied by the required rate, then there will be a residual left over after the subtraction. A division manager would be evaluated on the residual left over from all his projects combined.

Choosing the right profitability measure to monitor your financial objectives is not an easy task. Even though it is difficult for one return on investment measure to provide effective evaluation of the performance of both a manager and the organisation, it is even harder to use that same measure of performance to motivate managers to act in accordance with the best interests of the organisation. Despite this, many organisations continue to use just one return on investment measure for the organisation and its managers. In attempting to make the measure serve multiple roles, the measures used are often so complex that they are difficult to understand. This can cause managerial behaviour inconsistent with the mission of the organisation.

HOW TO USE ECONOMIC VALUE ADDED AS A MANAGEMENT TOOL

You have heard the expression it takes money to make money. It is true. Without capital from your shareholders, you would not be in business. Accordingly, it makes sense to measure your performance in a way that is meaningful to shareholders. The discussion in this chapter so far has concentrated on traditional yardsticks for measuring performance. Financial measures can be extremely useful, but they have their limitations:

▶ There is only anecdotal evidence of a consistent relationship between these measures and share price.

▶ Most measures do not take into account all the costs associated with obtaining the capital needed to operate and expand an organisation.

Economic value added (EVA) is a measure that is being adopted by some of the world's leading companies in their balanced scorecards. These companies are keen to maximise long-term growth and profitability (like Coca-Cola and AT&T) by questioning whether they create real wealth for their shareholders or not. In particular, EVA requires an organisation to look hard at its core strengths to determine whether the organisation is generating returns greater than the cost of capital. EVA assists an organisation to make wise, long-term investment decisions.

EVA can also be used as a goal-setting tool and to make decisions and gauge success. These are integral components of a successful measurement system. To reinforce the importance of EVA, remuneration systems could be directly linked to EVA results. Motivated by EVA, your people can perform their roles better and more efficiently.

According to EVA, an organisation creates value only when its profit exceeds the charge for the capital it uses. EVA can be expressed as a formula. It is the dollar amount arrived at by taking an organisation's operating profit after tax and then subtracting a charge for the use of the capital needed to generate that profit. It looks like this:

	Operating Revenue
Less	Operating Expenses
Is equal to	Earnings before Interest and Tax (EBIT)
Less	Tax
Is equal to	Profit after Tax (PAT)
Less	Capital Charge
Is equal to	**Economic Value Added (EVA)**

By way of illustration, imagine your organisation borrows $1,000,000 from the bank for a year. The interest rate on the loan is 10%, which amounts to $100,000 in interest. You take that $1,000,000 and invest it in the Australian Stock Market. At the end of one year your business earns an after-tax profit of 17%, or $170,000. Take the $170,000 earnings from your investment and subtract the $100,000 capital charge and you have the EVA, $70,000.

EVA—A tool for managing your business

EVA can help an organisation manage its business in the following ways:

▶ EVA steers investments into business areas which generate returns above the cost of capital required for the investments. EVA provides a conceptual framework for decisions about equipment purchases, marketing campaigns and acquisitions. EVA provides the answers better than EBIT. Under EBIT, good investment opportunities can be rejected if they're judged by whether EBIT is increased instead of by whether they can earn their cost of capital, since capital is not even considered. Using EVA, if an investment will return more than the cost of capital, it is a good one.

▶ EVA promotes the achievement of internal operational efficiencies *without* the investment of more capital (e.g. productivity gains, reduced cycle times, client service initiatives, astute purchasing and expense management).

▶ Business activities that do not produce a sufficient return on capital can be targeted for corrective action.

Linking EVA to compensation systems

The adaptive nature of balanced scorecards makes many organisations keen to link their scorecards to their incentive system. EVA-based incentives can be structured to motivate employees to take actions that will increase the long-term value of the organisation. When bonuses are based on EVA, both employees and shareholders participate in the organisation's success.

You want your employees to participate with you in the learning process. If you link incentives to the scorecard in the early stages, then they will assume you got the measures right and they will maximise along those dimensions.[38] With an EVA bonus plan, there is plenty of incentive opportunity. The plan pays an incremental bonus for every dollar of economic value added above an established level of EVA performance.

Employees add the value

Adding value begins with your people. Each person in an organisation can make a contribution to improving EVA performance by working on the drivers. For example:

▶ **Generate revenues**. Ask the question: what can I do to increase sales revenue?

▶ **Identify internal operating inefficiencies**. Ask the question: what can I do to ensure that the organisation operates more efficiently?

▶ **Find superior ways to use your time at work**. Do you spend time performing tasks that do not add value? If so, what can you do that would be more productive?

S UMMARY

World-class organisations put the shareholder first. From the financial dimension, these organisations use tools such as sales, profits, return on shareholders' equity, return on assets and return on net assets. In addition, firms using the balanced scorecard are tracking common size measures, liquidity measures, efficiency measures, solvency, profitability measures and EVA. You need your shareholders to be in business. Accordingly, the balanced scorecard monitors your performance in a way that is meaningful to shareholders.

A sample scorecard and case studies

A SAMPLE SCORECARD

World-class organisations integrate the best of the value-adding competencies of all the economic actors to yield a leaner, more flexible, dynamic organisation. A sample scorecard may look something like this one.

STRATEGIES	GOALS	MEASURES
Client		
	Client retention	Client loyalty
	Average client account size	Long-lasting client relationship
	Market share	
Internal business processes		
	Time to market	20% improvement in
	Capacity utilisation	manufacturing cycle time
	Unplanned downtime	To be responsive to sudden crises
		Safety
Innovation		
	Number of cross-functional transfers (to and from)	Cross-functional teamwork
	Percentage of sale from new products	New product as percentage of total sales
	Number of employee suggestions received and implemented	Ideas suggested vs implemented
Financial		
	Earnings	To improve profit before
	Market analysis	abnormals by 30% over
	Cash flow	8 years
	Contribution per employee	To increase market share locally by 5% in 5 years

TABLE 15

Key capability model

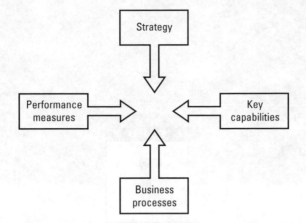

The scorecard should be based on the key capabilities and processes required to realise the strategy. An organisation's key capabilities are those skills that create client value and which provide a competitive advantage. The business processes are the internal workings of the business and should act as vehicles which deliver the capabilities to provide client value, and which must be cross-functional.

If an organisation's strategy is complete client satisfaction, then one key capability would be excellent client service. The internal processes which deliver that capability are knowledgeable, caring, personable and competent employees. The internal measures designed to capture the business' execution of the strategy are complaints resolution time, telephone response speed, product delivery times, inaccuracies in documentation and queue length. See Table 15 above.

POTTERSGROVE

IRON LTD

Organisation information

Pottersgrove Iron is a diversified miner and distributor of iron ore. The business unit accountable for the distribution of iron ore is known as 'Pottersgrove'. Pottersgrove is one of about a dozen companies in Australia competing in the iron ore distribution market, and while Pottersgrove does not have the lion's share of the world market, the organisation is considered by capital markets to be well-managed and an organisation that delivers world-class output. The strategic direction of Pottersgrove is to develop distribution networks in the Asia Pacific region.

Pottersgrove sells its iron ore through a number of long-standing agents who supply local iron ore markets. Pottersgrove depends on its excellent relations with the distributors who serve to promote Pottersgrove's products to end users and also receive feedback from the end users about different 'grades' of iron ore that they desire from time to time.

Pottersgrove knows that one of the critical factors underpinning its long-term competitive advantage depends on how much money the agents can make by promoting and selling its iron ore. If the profit from selling Pottersgrove's output is high, then the agents are more likely to promote its iron ore in preference to the iron ore of competitors, and Pottersgrove receives extensive feedback about future client needs. Pottersgrove has historically provided high-grade iron ore to the marketplace, but recent inroads by newly formed competitor distribution joint ventures have been eroding distributors' sales and profit margins. Pottersgrove has been successful in the past because of its track record of supplying a steady stream of iron ore to Asian-based infrastructure developers. In the first half of the 1990s, however, the low London Metals Exchange price, a corporate restructure program and cost blowouts have significantly retarded Pottersgrove's ability to offer competitively priced iron ore to its clients.

Research and development

The development of new technologies to support process improvements and to reduce Pottersgrove's reliance on human resources is a costly and uncertain process. Since 1989 corporate budgets have left the Research and Development business unit with less and less funds. With wages and development costs on the increase, this business unit has developed fewer and fewer 'new technologies' for Pottersgrove. The number of new patents filed per annum has dropped noticeably since 1989.

Manufacturing

Pottersgrove's manufacturing processes are considered among the best in the world. Management takes pride in the ability of the manufacturing operation to quickly and efficiently ramp up to produce enough iron ore to meet the needs of the biggest client. Pottersgrove also has the capability to produce small batches of custom-grade iron ore that clients require.

Performance measurement

Pottersgrove allows each of its business units to take control of their own reins, provided that all of the business units move in accordance with the company's vision. Pottersgrove sets high but achievable targets for its business units to meet. The targets are usually expressed in terms of return on investment, return on assets and economic value added. As a diversified organisation, Pottersgrove wants to cross-subsidise product development and downstream business units (in the short term) using funds generated from the most profitable business units. Financial reports are submitted to head office by each business unit every month. Henry Lloyd, Pottersgrove's Finance Director, meets each month with each business unit Managing Director to discuss the performance of the business unit for the preceding month.

Time for change: the balanced scorecard

Henry Lloyd is not convinced that his monthly review of business units from the monthly reports and his meeting with business unit heads adds to his awareness of how the organisation is performing in the way he would like. Most of the Managing Directors consistently complain that the targets have been set too high and that they are unachievable, unless adjusted downwards. The other heads argue for a change from the continual pressure to meet short-term financial targets when the nature of their businesses is to achieve high returns over the long term. Lloyd regards the balanced scorecard model as an attractive way to balance short-term financial objectives and long-run corporate goals.

Lloyd brought the model to the attention of Pottersgrove's Chief Executive, Isaac Newman. Newman shared Lloyd's enthusiasm for the model and felt that a balanced scorecard would give business unit heads greater scope in how they measured and presented their results of operations to corporate head office. He was very keen about introducing a methodology to make business unit heads accountable for improving the long-term performance of their unit.

Before long, Newman instructed Lloyd to issue a memorandum to all of Pottersgrove's managing directors. The memo had a clear message: to read the précis about the balanced scorecard, to design a scorecard for your business unit and to be ready to front up at head office in three months to present and defend the newly developed scorecard to Newman. The memo stated that Newman was only interested in looking at 'hard measures' but that each business unit was at liberty to develop a measurement set of soft measures for internal reporting requirements.

Nigel Terison, the managing director of Pottersgrove, received Lloyd's memo together with the précis on the balanced scorecard and was concerned. Terison welcomed a model that was more responsive to his business unit, but was unsure about how much freedom Newman and Lloyd would give him to develop his own scorecard.

Terison took a few minutes to translate the vision of his business unit, and to identify the key business strategies of his business. The vision was: '*Pottersgrove endeavours to be the leading distributor of iron ore in Asia Pacific*'.

The business strategies were:

1. **Manage Pottersgrove's assets**
   ▶ Minimise the cost of executing its existing business.
   ▶ Maximise the return on assets.
   ▶ Maximise economic value added.

2. **Satisfy client needs**

▶ Minimise delivery times.

▶ Meet demand requirements every time.

▶ Administer sales efficiently.

3. **Manage operations**

▶ Minimise defective products.

▶ Maximise volume of high grade iron ore.

▶ Maximise cost/volume ratio.

4. **People development**

▶ Workforce training.

▶ Next-generation workforce development.

Terison wrote a memorandum to Richard Blake, the Chief Financial Officer of his business unit. In it Terison instructed Blake to set up a taskforce to design a balanced scorecard. Terison attached to his memo the précis on the scorecard and a copy of the note he had written about Pottersgrove's vision and business objectives. Blake was required to be ready to discuss a draft scorecard with Terison within 45 days.

Blake had a very busy schedule. He received Terison's memo but because he and all of the other divisional managers were busy, he would not be able to discuss the model with anyone until the next General Manager's conference. Blake issued a memo to all of the other General Managers (attaching Terison's memo) and specifically requested that at least two hours of the next conference be spent discussing measures for the scorecard.

At the General Manager's Conference, Blake found that all but two of the 12 General Managers had read his memo and the attachments. Each of these had several measures which they believed were key indicators of the business strategies set out by Terison. Blake was well placed to develop a draft scorecard. Blake felt that more value could be gained from the process if Terison and each General Manager set aside half a day offsite to reach consensus on the measures. The earliest Blake could organise for Terison and all of the General Managers to be present was in a month.

Blake sent a memo to Terison requesting that their progress meeting be replaced by a half-day conference. Terison agreed that the conference was a good idea. Accordingly, Blake issued a memo to the other General Managers advising them of the conference.

On the day of the conference (held offsite so that the taskforce could operate uninterrupted by day-to-day issues) Blake arrived early and wrote up on a whiteboard the measures previously identified. Breakfast was to be supplied at 8.30am. Everybody save for three General Managers attended the session. Terison was interrupted by phone calls several times and had to leave early. Others were interrupted with urgent calls.

The group managed to reach consensus on the measures which Terison would present to Newman. Targets were set at 12-month intervals for the next five years. Improvement plans were also identified.

Blake had one further session with Terison one week before Terison's appearance before Newman.

After 24 months of using the balanced scorecard, Lloyd put substantially more credibility in the monthly reports prepared by each business unit. He now believes he has the information he needs to make the decisions to lead the company to its ultimate destination. So too is Terison managing the business unit according to the balanced scorecard framework. Terison has identified workforce training as one of the key factors which will ultimately drive superior financial performance. Terison intends to increase next year's training budget by an unprecedented amount.

PUBLIC TRANSPORT

BODY

Organisation information

The Public Transport Body is a quasi government department of one of Australia's state governments. The Body operates the public transport network of the relevant state and is directed by the state government to produce a profit at year end. Although the Body is governed by an Act of Parliament, it enjoys a significant degree of autonomy to set policy (the minister has the last say), regulate employee levels, purchase and dispose of trains and other infrastructure, make investments in the property market and negotiate contracts with preferred suppliers, such as suppliers of electricity.

The Public Transport Body is divided into three main business units: trains, buses and networks. As their names suggest, the trains and buses divisions are responsible for generating profits in each of these service offerings, whilst the network division is accountable for developing the functional infrastructure of the organisation (e.g. purchasing new trains and buses as required) and improving the support infrastructure such as electricity network. In addition, a number of other divisions exist and these are in the service areas of human resources and accounting.

Strategic direction of public transport

In recent years, the Public Transport Body has undergone considerable reorganisation. In particular, improvements in work practices and the introduction of new technology has resulted in less 'shop floor' staff. In addition, process improvement and process re-engineering projects have streamlined the number of management positions. The new head of the Public Transport Body, Melissa Watson, is concerned that the financial reporting system cannot deliver the information she needs to make the kind of strategic decisions which the government hired her to perform.

To add to that, the Body has delivered a net loss every year for the last five years. Her job is to turn the organisation around, and bring it into profit within three years.

Monthly reports

At the end of the first month in her new position, Melissa Watson met with the divisional heads of the trains, buses and network divisions and listened to their feedback on the performance of their divisions over the last month.

Performance measurement

After only a little time, it became clear to Watson that, despite the obvious inter-relationships between the three divisions, there was little communication between them. Moreover, the only measures which all three heads presented to Watson were financial measures. It was clear that the trains division was the poor performer of the group.

Peter James, the head of the trains division, explained that the poor performance was due to changing views of consumers about using their cars that was leading consumers away from trains and causing the loss to the division.

When Watson asked for the graphs on consumer satisfaction levels with trains, James said that he believed consumer confidence in the system was low, but could not present any hard data to support that view.

Over the course of the next month, Watson was concerned about identifying a solution that would give her the information she needed to make strategic decisions about the business, and at the same time improve the level of communication between departments. Watson had heard about the balanced scorecard performance measurement system from reading management journals, and, after considering alternative lines of inquiry, decided that the scorecard was the best option for the Public Transport Body.

Time for change: The balanced scorecard

At the next monthly meeting, Watson used the leadership of her role to start the design of the balanced scorecard. She explained the concept to the divisional heads, and they seemed eager to give the model a run.

Watson presented the heads with the vision of the organisation, which she had formulated recently. The vision of the Body was: *The Public Transport Body aims to offer the preferred mode of transport to consumers across the state.*

The business strategies were:

1. **Improve train passenger satisfaction levels**
   ▶ Maximise the comfort to passengers during the ride.
   ▶ Minimise the incidence of delayed and cancelled trains.
   ▶ Maximise passenger value.
   ▶ Administer sales efficiently.

2. **Improve the support infrastructure**
   ▶ Minimise the cost of electricity.
   ▶ Meet demand requirements every time.

3. **Manage operations**
   ▶ Maximise vehicle uptime.
   ▶ Maximise passenger levels on all vehicles.

4. **People development**
   ▶ Workforce training.
   ▶ Information technology workforce competency levels.

Watson then instructed each division head, in particular James, to develop goals, targets, improvement initiatives and measures over the next month. The heads then had to present their outcomes to Watson at the next monthly meeting.

When the next monthly meeting took place, Watson and the division heads reached substantial agreement on the form the goals and measures should take. The substantive content of the improvement initiatives had been outlined in broad terms. It was apparent to each person present, however, that the financial reporting system was incapable of delivering the information needed to measure the key drivers of performance. Everyone agreed that a new information reporting system would be expensive.

As it was, the financial reporting system was not year 2000 compliant, and an independent computer consultant confirmed that the cheapest option open to the Public Transport Body was to install a new system. Watson met with the Minster for Transport to obtain her approval for the new software package. After a period of two months, the Minister approved the funds necessary to install a new computer system.

After a tender process, Watson and divisional heads settled on a computer system which could deliver the information required. The staff would have to be trained in how to use the new system, and the software supplier agreed to provide this level of client service as part of the package.

Post installation of the new system, Watson had access at her monthly meetings along with the divisional heads to key financial data that was complemented with softer measures of the Body's performance. Consequently, Watson was able for the first time to see how consumer satisfaction levels are affected by the percentage of buses and trains that arrived late or not at all. The divisional heads had improved understanding of how a decision in their area of operation could affect the performance in another area of the organisation. Over the next six months, communication levels improved between the divisional heads. In turn, they encouraged their staff to develop cross-functional skill competencies.

It is still early days for the organisation in assessing whether Watson's vision of the direction as the preferred supplier of transport facilities will pay dividends for the Body, but with the greater emphasis on lead performance indicators, Watson and other decision makers are able to make decisions which can maximise the value to the Public Transport Body.

TRUDY'S DRESS SHOP

Organisation information

Trudy's Ladieswear sells a wide variety of ladies clothes, ranging from evening wear to fashion accessories. Trudy Thomas is the store owner and over the last five years has expanded her business from a single shop front to having a shop at most major shopping centres in Melbourne, Australia. This was made possible when Trudy obtained extra cash from the bank by mortgaging her home. Trudy now has seven ladies clothes stores operating under the banner of Trudy's Ladieswear.

When Trudy first opened shop, she operated her business as a sole proprietor. As she expanded, she hired sales staff and is now a proud employer of 52 staff.

Financial performance

Since commencing business, Trudy has changed accountants several times and now believes she has 'found the right accountant' in Roger Penfold. In the past, when Trudy went to her accountant to complete the company's tax return, she would also obtain advice about how she could improve the performance of the business. After each review, all Trudy ever seemed to receive from her accountant was a list of financial measures indicating areas of improvement, but nothing else. Because she relied heavily on the sales skills of her staff for her bottom-line financial result, she wanted to monitor employee satisfaction levels so that she could implement corrective action if need be. The accountants told her to measure the sales revenue earned by each staff person.

Performance measurement

Trudy now spends most of her time travelling to her suppliers selecting fabrics and accessories which she wants to stock. When she is in the office, she is reviewing a number of reports her store managers prepare regularly.

The performance reports contain a balanced set of financial and non-financial measures so that Trudy can take proactive action when necessary, anticipate peaks and troughs in demand, and implement corrective action when something goes wrong.

It wasn't always this way. Until Roger suggested the balanced scorecard approach, Trudy's monthly performance reports consisted of a profit and loss statement, balance sheet for each store and cash-flow statement. Trudy felt that the reports told her nothing about her business. Admittedly, she knew which stores were underperforming others; but she had no way of identifying the causes. In most cases, Trudy would jump on the phone and place a call to the store manager whose store was lagging behind the others. This process was time consuming, the store managers lost their confidence because they saw her phone call as a negative reinforcement of their performance. In one instance, Trudy feels that a similar incident was the principal cause of one of her long-serving staff members leaving the company. Trudy felt that there had to be a better solution.

When Roger Penfold filled in for another accountant, Trudy took the opportunity to seek counsel on ways to manage her business more efficiently. Roger suggested the balanced scorecard concept to her, gave her some materials to read and asked her to call again if she wanted to talk more on the subject.

The balanced scorecard approach

Trudy returned to Roger one month later. She had already formulated the vision statement of her business, and had written down several strategic objectives for the four dimensions: client, internal business process, learning and growth, and financial. Roger and Trudy fine-tuned those strategic objectives, giving them a three-year outlook. They then developed goals for Trudy's business to achieve over the next year in line with those objectives. Each store was assigned targets. The targets were based on the previous financial performance of each store. In addition, each store was assigned improvement initiatives in order to achieve the targets.

Over two more sessions, Trudy and Roger developed the performance measures. Roger compiled the balanced scorecard report card to replace the original monthly performance reports.

Trudy held a quarterly meeting with her store managers, briefed them on the new approach she was taking for the company and the changes to the reporting information. The meeting also doubled as a training session so that each manager understood what was required of them, and how they could find the information they needed.

Improved outcomes

After 16 months using the scorecard system, Trudy has considerably more confidence that she is receiving the information she requires each month to effectively lead her business, whenever she is overseas buying stock or in her office.

Now when one store is underperforming the others, Trudy can see whether the cause is low consumer satisfaction, low staff morale, market factors or related to poor stock on hand. One store was constantly underperforming the others, so rather than incurring the expense of retrenching the staff in that store together with hiring and training new staff, she 'transferred' each staff member from that store one at a time to work for one month at the best performing store. The staff members returned with improved sales skills, and in 1997 that store was the second-best performer of any store in Trudy's business.

DESIGNING AND IMPLEMENTING YOUR BALANCED SCORECARD

Evaluating your current performance measurement system

The greatest of faults is to be conscious of none. THOMAS CARLYLE

Daring as it is to investigate the unknown,

even more so is it to question the known. KASPER

The balanced scorecard allows an organisation to answer four critical questions: How do our clients see us? How can we add value to the organisation? How do we look to our shareholders? What must we excel at? Planning, designing and then implementing a balanced scorecard is a strategic investment. It requires as much careful analysis as a decision to invest in new information technology. The first stage is to review the effectiveness of your existing performance system. This chapter identifies five common tell-tale signs of a deficient performance measurement system and the seven rules of successful performance measurement. Once you have evaluated your organisation's performance measurement system, you will be in a position to decide whether you should move to the next stage: designing your own balanced scorecard.

DEFICIENT PERFORMANCE MEASUREMENT SYSTEMS

Organisations should constantly appraise their performance measurement systems. This will flush out any deficiencies with the system. In turn, these deficiencies can be evaluated and, if they are so fundamental to the proper performance of the system, then some consideration should be given to designing and interpreting a balanced scorecard.

Your prices are competitive, but demand for your products is lagging

Imagine that you are reviewing your copy of your organisation's monthly financial report. After fifteen minutes of reading, what have you noticed? Costs are down, productivity is high, employee morale is good, prices are competitive, product quality has never been better, but client demand is as high as demand for umbrellas on a sunny day!

If what you measure is what you manage, then this performance measurement system does not measure the key drivers of business performance. Were the clients' expectations met last month? Will they be met next month and the month after that? Do you know what your clients expect from you as their preferred supplier?

Take time out to establish exactly what your clients' priorities are, and try to learn from them what you need to do in order to be their ideal supplier. As soon as the goals are established, the measures will follow. There is no difficulty in identifying measures. Rather, the difficulty is in deciding on the most appropriate ones.

Benchmarking systems are a fundamental requirement of improving the competitive advantage of all businesses today. Chapter 11, Benchmarking Your Performance Measures, covers this topic in detail. The purpose of a benchmarking system should be to direct managers' attention to the development of imperative corporate behaviour geared to inspiring best practices goals.

You stop preparing a performance report and nobody notices

A number of reasons may explain why nobody notices when you decide to no longer prepare a performance measurement report. The single most requisite characteristic of a performance report is that it must contain information.

A report may be improperly prepared such that it fails to concisely, clearly and effectively communicate performance information to managers. In addition, a report can be prepared too often for top executives to gain a broad enough understanding of trends affecting the organisation. An effective strategic performance measurement system reports the performance of the organisation relative to its specific goals and delivers that information without causing sensory saturation to decision-makers; hence they can stay focused on the 'bigger picture'.

The internal reporting system could be operating sub-optimally. High turnover of managers often results in staff preparing reports used by the former manager but not by the new one. Accordingly, it is essential for managers in receipt of regular performance reports to communicate their performance reporting requirements to their staff. As a result, duplicated work effort should reduce.

More typically, nobody notices that a report has not been prepared if what it contains is not information at all. The fast pace of technological change and structural global market reshuffling means that the competitive advantage of today's world-class organisation depends on flexible and adaptable internal performance measurement systems. In traditional organisations, strategic measurement systems are built around financial accounting data. The problem is that while an organisation adapts to its external environment, performance measures can remain static. Strategic measurement should operate at a level above the specific project to support and facilitate organisation-wide goal congruency. The attainment of goal congruency is compromised when the measurement system is either outdated or too inflexible to adapt to the environment in which the organisation operates.

Even if the report does contain information, nobody might notice that it has not been prepared because the intended recipient obtains the information from elsewhere. For example, suppose that an organisation's client strategy is to sell 80% of all products to one market. The organisation may track its performance on the basis of the percentage of 'sales' to that market. Sales can be defined as goods *shipped* during the month, and goods actually *invoiced* to clients. For management reporting purposes, both measures produce the same information. If staff are required to prepare reports on the basis of both definitions of 'sales', then there is probably wasteful duplication of output. Needless to say, this should be eliminated.

The balanced scorecard emphasises cross-functional reports and promotes broad vertical and horizontal knowledge within an organisation. When managers use measures that inform them about the organisation's performance, all other similarly based reports can be eliminated.

All the measures say the business strategy is working save for profit

Some organisations turn out sub-optimal profits or even losses, even though the host of measures on which they rely point to a blue sky. Such organisations operate TQM (i.e. total quality management) or time-based management systems and utilise non-financial performance measures to track quality and design efficiencies. These organisations have reduced design and manufacturing cycle times and can offer superior delivery times.

TQM, time-based management programs and soft measures are priceless programs, but they must be consistent with an organisation's strategy. For any of these programs to increase shareholder wealth, managers must recognise that these tools are only conduits for executing the ultimate *raison d'être* of the organisation.

Integrated operations systems are the strategic link between those programs and real bottom-line success. The balanced scorecard complements the integrated operations systems in a way which reflects the vision of an organisation over time. The reason lies in the fact that a balanced set of performance measures can serve an organisation's long term goals, which TQM and time-based management programs do not.

You have used the same performance measures for years

If what is managed is what gets controlled, then either bottom-line profits improve or nothing happens. A well-designed performance measurement system is dynamic. It is flexible. Old measures become obsolete and are replaced by new ones. A system of that calibre fosters change because the organisation has the information to assess and reassess its goals and strategic direction.

The four dimensions of your measurement system are not integrated

Few organisations have linked the disparate elements of the measurement system so that the effects of actions in one area of the organisation show up in other areas. Changes in levels of resource use, product offerings, taxation policies, financial structure, organisation structure and research and development expenditures are often initiated by managers without regard to the effect on the change to other areas of the organisation and on the goals. The effect of any change, however, is felt by all functions, and any change influences the measures in all functions' performance measurement systems.[39]

Accordingly, world-class organisations are aligning their performance measures in one function to other measures in other functions. When the correct measures are in place decisions can be made to synchronise actions in one area of the organisation with the achievement of the organisation's shared vision.[40]

SEVEN RULES OF SUCCESSFUL PERFORMANCE MEASUREMENT

There is no undertaking more hazardous or more uncertain of its success than the introduction of a new order of things, because all organisations have internal critics who utilise the existing system as their comfort zone. Similarly, clients demand improved quality, such as shorter delivery times, cheaper prices and greater responsiveness. Performance measures are the most direct means for identifying areas of actual and potential improvement. When the improvement initiatives are linked to targets, organisations can maximise along these lines. Managers who lack important information can operate blindly. Effective performance measurement in a world-class organisation should be guided by the following seven rules.

Rule 1: Performance measurement must be value based

Performance measures can help managers to understand what is important to the stakeholders. The stakeholders of each organisation are not always the same, but typically include the staff, clients, shareholders, suppliers, government, financiers, the accountants and lawyers. A value-based measure can monitor the factors which will drive value to stakeholders over time. It is up to the organisation to focus the attention of staff on the improvement in the underlying processes. A value-based focus means that the organisation is directed to achieve a strategic plan, which has *measurable results*.

Rule 2: Performance measures must influence the achievement of strategic objectives

Inadequately designed or poorly implemented performance measurement systems can create incentives which can over-emphasise short-term results. Suppose a manager's chance of promotion depends upon her short-term performance. That manager may weigh effort towards the achievement of short-term improvements in performance. This means that there could be an under-investment by that manager in innovation, quality improvements and training initiatives for her division.

Over-emphasis on the short-term can also lead to lower profits in the long term. As a corollary, this can lower the net present value of an organisation, which is one of the worst things to happen to an organisation contemplating an asset sell-off. Organisations should be careful to ensure that performance measures are designed to improve behaviour, and are not susceptive to manipulation and distortion by those whose remuneration might be affected by them. Your performance measurement system should be designed to improve the life line of the organisation. To achieve this, a long-term, multi-dimensional approach is required.

Rule 3: Performance measures must not operate in a vacuum

An organisation's vision, values and guiding principles must be developed and visibly promoted by its leaders. A world-class organisation has to change both culturally and structurally before performance measures can operate successfully. To guide these changes, a clear and unambiguous direction is needed from the top layer of the organisation. Managers must demonstrate genuine support for the performance measurement system if they are to create a positive attitude for organisational change. Consistency is a key element in management actions and behaviours. Line managers must send out the same message to everybody in the organisation.

Rule 4: Performance measures must not be sold as a self-contained solution

Performance measures do not of themselves produce higher levels of client satisfaction, effectiveness, efficiency and quality. These results are achieved through decisions to reallocate or reassign resources, to improve internal business processes and changing task priorities. But, performance measurement does provide some of the information necessary to redirect resources. That information does not replace judgement and professional experience; rather it should *complement* them in the decision-making process.

Rule 5: Rewards must be linked to performance

The way to people's hearts and minds is through their wallets. An organisation's management system shapes its values. If you want people to share your values, you have to specifically measure and reward them *for exhibiting those values*. If you do otherwise, then your staff will probably be confused about the importance of the values you espouse because they do not experience positive reinforcements for adopting them.

Gaining a competitive advantage in the marketplace today requires a structured process—one that aligns resources to objectives and key performance measures. Experience has shown that people's behaviour is directly linked to the criteria by which they are measured. This is particularly true when their remuneration package is tied to certain performance measures.

Rule 6: Performance measures must be comparable

The information obtained from the measures must enable comparisons to be made. Measurement performed in a vacuum is like not measuring at all. An organisation's performance can be compared with a goal or target, and to other organisations if benchmarking information is available.

Rule 7: Performance measures must provide a balanced view

There is no single performance indicator that can provide you with a universal snapshot of the organisation. A small set of indicators provides a balanced perspective. Seldom do people understand that an organisation consists of an interrelated series of dependent processes for a common purpose.[41] Actions taken to achieve the common purpose by one resource may impact negatively on other resources. Only by linking the performance measurement system between organisational layers and across functions can your organisation ensure that its processes are being used effectively.[42]

SUMMARY

Not every performance measurement system allows an organisation to answer the four critical questions: How do our clients see us? How can we add value to the organisation? What do the shareholders think? What can we excel at? Planning, designing and implementing a balanced scorecard begins with a review of the effectiveness of the existing system. This chapter has identified various common features of a performance measurement system that can pinpoint problems with an existing system, demonstrating where it needs repair.

Designing your balanced scorecard

1. Scope the project

2. Define your vision

3. Determine your objectives

4. Determine your goals

5. Establish performance measures

6. Establish targets and improvement initiatives

7. Identify accountable parties

8. Predict the results

People who constantly live in the past are afraid of the present. P. K. Shaw

Destiny is no matter of chance. It is a matter of choice: it is not a thing

to be waited for, it is a thing to be achieved. WILLIAM JENNING BRYAN

Until now, the focus has been primarily on *why* your organisation requires a balanced scorecard and *what* the balanced scorecard can do for your organisation to help it achieve competitive advantage in the marketplace. In this chapter, a broader view of the scorecard is given and the development of a balanced scorecard is considered. As you have seen in Chapter 1, every organisation is different from the next. Designing the balanced scorecard system should be a flexible process tailored specifically to meet an organisation's requirements. Some organisations may choose to implement a complete scorecard, while others can start off using it as a pilot program, gradually building a fully integrated scorecard as the benefits emerge.

The balanced scorecard has been quickly endorsed by the business world. It is easy to see the value of a focused set of performance measurements. However, an effective balanced scorecard is more than a limited list of measures seen through its four dimensions. A good balanced scorecard integrates your strategy with its tactical execution.

The first step in designing a balanced scorecard is to translate the organisation's vision into clear strategies. The measures are then linked to those strategies. Not just any measures, but the ones that best track the organisation's progress towards its strategies. This requires good planning and breakthrough thinking by the organisation's leaders. A final balanced scorecard is ultimately obtained by funnelling into the process the input of senior managers. When the scorecard has reached the finished product stage, it is implemented throughout the organisation. This chapter contains an eight-step methodology for designing a scorecard (see Table 16). The methodology has been designed primarily for organisations which have over 100 staff. For smaller organisations, this process can be streamlined.

1. SCOPE THE PROJECT

The design process begins when you identify the business unit of the organisation for which the scorecard is required. The balanced scorecard works most effectively for a business unit that is a separate reporting entity (i.e. provides products or services to external clients, has its own internal business processes and utilises financial performance measures).

You must also define what the organisation hopes to gain from the

TABLE 16

Balanced scorecard design process

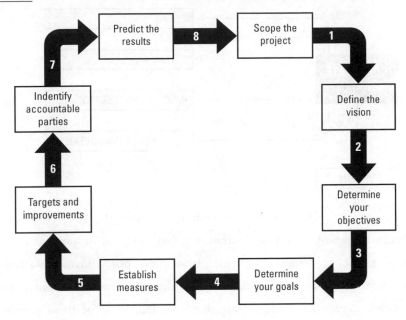

introduction of a balanced scorecard. Many organisations have the same goals in mind. In the end, the rationale of each organisation depends on a variety of factors such as competitive position, competitive environment, organisational culture and financial position.

2. DEFINE YOUR VISION

A vision should give your organisation a sense of purpose and direction. The question 'What business are we in?' provides the focus to determine the vision statement. Too often visions are poorly defined. A well-articulated vision statement can remedy any lack of clarity and specificity and can serve as a template to guide the organisation to its desired future. Vision statements are actionable visions![43]

One technique for defining an organisation's vision involves the appointment of:

1. a balanced scorecard facilitator who is an independent consultant or one of the leaders of the organisation; and

2. a Scorecard Design Team to manage the design of the new system.

Once the Scorecard Design Team is in place, the facilitator sends a group of the

TABLE 17   **Balanced scorecard design objectives**

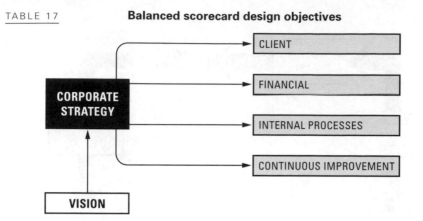

most senior managers a folder containing documents which explain the organisation's current vision and strategies (i.e. various mission and vision statements, corporate strategies, strategic plans, annual plans, financial statements, intranet, board papers and media releases). Also attached is background material on the balanced scorecard. The facilitator allows enough time for these persons to review the material. At a workshop, the facilitator then leads the group to reach consensus on what they think the vision of the organisation is. The outcome is often a richer, clearer statement of the organisation's purposes.

3. DETERMINE YOUR OBJECTIVES

Although you have defined the vision statement, a vision is too broad to direct your client, financial, internal business process and learning strategies. Vision statements must now be translated into a set of strategic objectives. The facilitator can do this by allowing the group of managers to define the factors critical to your organisation's success by asking the questions: If you realise your vision, how will you differ –

1. To your clients?
2. In your ability to continuously improve?
3. To your shareholders?
4. In your internal business processes?

Objectives are very important because they set the direction for all processes in the balanced scorecard. Table 17 shows the translation of an organisation's vision into four objectives. Objectives are the warm and fuzzy expressions that should form the mindset for all who are involved in the system. Objectives require a five- to -eight-year outlook. Smaller organisations can do with a shorter outlook, such as three years. Examples of objectives include:

▶   To provide good haircuts with superior client service (client).

▶   To be the safest taxi company (learning and growth).

▶   To offer the most competitive fares (financial).

▶   To produce user-friendly washing machines (internal business processes).

The choice of objectives sets the strategic direction of an organisation. Accordingly, objectives are the driving force in the selection of performance measures. In the end, what is done and measured must tie back to the objectives. For instance, to achieve its internal business process objective, a washing machine manufacturer will need to research client needs. The measures could relate to inbound calls from clients asking for help with using their new machines and results from later surveys.

Objectives should be selected carefully. If you can pick something you are sure you would succeed at, that choice probably should be your number one objective.

ICI Fibres (now Orica) has rethought its objectives. ICI Fibres found that a key business issue in any business performance management project was that the project needed to be driven by business needs and the dynamics of the management process needed to be understood. This case study highlights a number of key issues, among them: the need to effectively manage corporate change; to create a culture of accountability and to run a more flexible organisation able to deal swiftly with changing business opportunities. The issue is not just about financial or non-financial data, but about communicating all types of information throughout the organisation.[44]

4. DETERMINE YOUR GOALS

Be sure to differentiate between unrealistic and realistic goals. It is preferable to establish realistic goals (ones you have a reasonable chance of attaining). Goals have a three- to -five-year outlook. The goals which you ultimately select must be capable of realising your objectives. Another consideration that might help to set goals is benchmarking, which informs you of how well competitors are doing with similar processes. Chapter 11 considers benchmarking in detail.

Below are four 'rules' which you can use as a rough guide to choosing the right goals.

Rule 1. Use the numbers to help people improve, not to judge people.

Mathematicians have studied physical phenomena for years to understand and model how things work. Consequently, statistical methods have been developed that everyone working with performance measures should understand. Two main aspects of statistical methods deal with statistical distributions and statistical control.

It is important for the Scorecard Design Team to understand statistical concepts on variation, including statistical distributions and statistical control. In addition, the Scorecard Design Team should clearly understand the concept of 'tampering' with a process. Adjusting a process when you should not is tampering.

Rule 2. Learn to understand variation. You can be more effective.

One way of visualising variation is through a demonstration. Staff perform the operations in the system you provide them. They are given the procedures to follow. Managers are accountable for the system. If a change is required in the system, the change can only be made by managers. This natural pattern of variation shows what the process is capable of doing. If it is not preserved, you look for a special cause.

A key concept is that you must study the pattern of variation. If it is controlled, meaning observations fall seemingly at random within some overall natural pattern, then the process is probably performing as it should. Managers are accountable for improving a controlled process. If it is uncontrolled, then special causes of variation are present. The staff ought to be able to identify these special causes because of their closeness to the process.

Rule 3. Only persons with authority can improve a controlled process.

When people do not understand variation, many things can happen:

1. trends are identified when none is present;
2. trends are not identified when there are trends;
3. employees blame or credit others for things over which others have no control;
4. past performance cannot be understood; and
5. future plans cannot be made.

Any time you see common-cause variation and make a process adjustment to correct for this variation, you increase the variation in your process. You make it worse. The discussion in Chapter 6 on the tendency of financial measures to drive managers to perform in the short term only is an instance of tampering. For a manager or supervisor to react to normal process variation and expect explanations or corrective actions is wasteful. 'Last month there were six instances of machine breakdowns. This month there were eight. Why are breakdowns up 30 percent?'

Rule 4. Ignorance of variation is no excuse.

Your newly devised goals should encourage you to act. Worthwhile goals are to communicate more with clients, to better understand your processes and to promote teamwork. In your readiness to meet your goals, you must remember tampering.

Suppose product defects have been a problem in your organisation for some time. One of your internal process goals is 'to have fewer than 10 defects per 1,000 widgets in any month'. Typical actions that might flow from this are:

1. soliciting reasons why some months have more than 10 defective products per 1,000;

2. comparing information on months with more than 10 defective widgets with the information on the 'good' months;

3. celebrating for months where the goal is met; and

4. taking appropriate action on staff who produce defective products, or on line managers when goals are not met (e.g. retraining them).

While the goal of producing more high-quality products is good, any of these actions can be harmful. They can lead to fear, mistrust and a collapse in teamwork. Those who understand variation can make more informed decisions to identify the cause of the variation (e.g. training) that positively reinforce an organisation's goals.

5. ESTABLISH PERFORMANCE MEASURES

This step involves performing several activities that will continue to build the scorecard system. Each performance measure consists of a *unit of measure*, a *sensor* to measure or record the information, and a *frequency* with which the measurements are made. To develop a measure, the Scorecard Design Team, headed by the facilitator, can:

- translate 'if we realise our vision, how will we differ to …' into a measure;
- identify the information that will generate the measure;
- determine where to locate it;
- identify the sensor that will collect the information for the measures; and
- determine how often to make the measures.

This is probably the most complex step in the methodology.

Translate into performance measures

Having identified precisely what you want to know about your organisation, you must now construct a measure. Performance measures should be chosen to tell you whether or not your organisation is achieving its goals. The facilitator could obtain the input of the managers who translated the vision into clear objectives earlier. A workshop is one medium by which to do this.

A good way for a facilitator to test a group's understanding of the measures they have chosen is to have them describe how it would display its results graphically. Have the group explain what type of graph it would use for each performance measure and how it would interpret the results. Usually, just seeing a performance measure displayed graphically can determine if it will provide the information needed. Doing this simple step now will help ensure that the group has chosen the right performance measures. Generating three or four measures per goal is sufficient.

Identify the data

The Scorecard Design Team needs to identify the data the organisation will need to generate the measures. It is difficult to measure performance if the needed data and data source have not been identified. For very simple processes with straightforward measures, this step may seem simple. It is likely that small businesses have simple processes to measure, but not always. However, very complex measures may require many data from a variety of sources. Rarely are measures generated from a single source. They usually consist of some combination of other data elements. When the Scorecard Design Team completes this activity, it should have a list of the data elements needed to generate the performance measures. In addition, the Scorecard Design Team should consider what, if any, computations or calculations must be performed with or on the data.

Locate the data

The Scorecard Design Team should determine *if* and *where* the data exists. Often this activity is performed concurrently with the previous one.

Identify the sensors

By this point, the Scorecard Design Team has determined what raw data it requires, where it is located and where it will be collected. To proceed, it must determine how the data will be measured. A sensor is required to accomplish the measurement.

Sensors take many forms depending on what they are designed to measure. Sensors are the micrometer, thermometer, tape measure or computer, databases, log books, time sheets and spreadsheets. In some cases, the sensor takes a measurement and a person records the results. In other cases, only a person is capable of 'sensing' some phenomena and some other device is used to record the result. Many inspection activities can only be performed by people. There are also automated data collection systems or sensors that require no human intervention other than calibration or maintenance. Many manufacturing processes employ such sensors to detect, measure, and record the presence of non-standard products.

Determine how often to make measurements

How often should measurements be made? In a sense, there are two distinct types of measures taken when a performance measurement system is adopted. One type of measure is the performance measure itself. This measure is generally taken (calculated) and reported over some regular time interval. Often the unit of measure chosen as the performance measure contains or alludes to the frequency of measurement.

The other measure that should be addressed is that of the data itself. The frequency with which data are collected or measured may have a significant impact upon the interpretation of the performance measure. For some performance measures, this amounts to asking how much data is needed to make the measure valid or statistically significant. When the scorecard is implemented, each supervisor (if that is the authorised person) will have to determine how often measurements must be made (data taken) to ensure statistical significance and believable results.

6. ESTABLISH TARGETS AND IMPROVEMENT INITIATIVES

Now that your long-term goals are linked to your vision, you can close the single learning loop by linking your targets and improvement initiatives to your goals. Your target-setting technique should rely on industry best practices as the basis for setting your targets. In this way, managers can soundly set about implementing improvement initiatives. Targets have a one- to –three-year outlook (shorter for small businesses) compared with improvement initiatives which should take up to one year to implement.

7. IDENTIFY ACCOUNTABLE PARTIES

Who should be accountable for collecting the information, analysing and reporting actual performance, comparing actual performance with the goals, targets or improvement initiatives (as the case may be), determining if corrective action is necessary and then making changes? Accountability should be assigned to individuals commensurate with authority. This means that each accountable party should understand what their deliverables are and who has the authority to implement changes if performance falls too far short of the goals. To hold someone accountable in the absence of authority prevents them from performing their role and creates the risk of unjustified blame.

Establish data collection processes

The facilitator needs to supervise the information collection process to determine if the information is being collected properly and if people are performing tasks assigned to them. In large organisations, the facilitator will need to delegate the task of working this out to a number of personnel.

Establish your data collection system

As obvious as it sounds, a system is required that is capable of collecting and storing your measurements. Most measures can be easily entered into a computer database. Whatever system is chosen, it should provide easy access and be understandable by those who are tasked with reviewing the data. Those tasked with performing the data collection should understand the data collection system, have the necessary forms at hand, be trained in the data collection and have access to instructions pertaining to the system.

The data collected needs to be accurate. Inaccurate data may give the wrong answer to your information questions. One of the most troublesome sources of error is called bias. It is important to understand bias and to allow for this during the development and implementation of the balanced scorecard.

8 . PREDICT THE RESULTS

The facilitator should now bring together the Scorecard Design Team and their subordinates in order to reach a final decision on the strategic performance measures. A manager's meeting is good for this purpose. The facilitator brings together the executives and the top layer of managers in the organisation, arranging them into at least five groups, preferably cross-functional ones. The purpose of the meeting, and it need last for no more than one day, is to obtain final agreement on:

▶ the vision;
▶ the strategic objectives;
▶ the goals;
▶ the performance drivers that link them;
▶ the targets for each of the proposed measures;
▶ the improvement initiatives;
▶ other important issues such as:
   (a) development of an implementation plan (including the ways the balanced scorecard could be implemented across the organisation); and
   (b) consideration of any reconfigurations to the IT system to support the new scorecard.

It is clear that across the board many people will have questions like: 'How is *this system* any better than the one we currently have?' 'What does it mean for the work of my role?' 'Where does it all lead to?' 'Why even bother?' And comments such as: 'I'll believe the benefits when I see them myself!' Or 'Not another system. Hasn't management got anything better to do with their time!'

Naturally, building commitment for the scorecard is as delicate a process as the implementation of all other organisation-wide systems, so it should be handled with care. One Australian car insurer, NRMA, implemented its continuous improvement program and involved everybody in the process. All employees were involved, not just quality people or management; the scorecard became part of the *'way we work'*. NRMA recognised that if it did not measure service performance or client satisfaction, then it would be very difficult to educate its staff on what is important, or give them feedback on their performance against its strategy. Measurement and facts are important to be able to plan properly to meet clients needs, now and in the future.[45]

The difficulty in reaching consensus is typical in large organisations, but consensus is vital if the balanced scorecard is to be successfully implemented. Ericsson Australia solved it by giving ownership of each of the measures to an executive manager. This meant that each executive manager would develop it and if they felt it was not meaningful, they would make a case.[46] Accordingly, it may be necessary to mediate the internal pressures within the organisation in order to maximise effectiveness for clients. Internal pressures can deter an organisation from reaping the rewards of its new system. Internal support for the balanced scorecard is vital so that improvements are quickly passed on to the clients.

SUMMARY

Even if at first glance the design of a balanced scorecard appears to be difficult or cumbersome this should not dissuade an organisation from its application. Rather than clinging to more mechanical frameworks, leaders can be better served by tending to strategy development and planning. Four elements are key here: treating planning and design as primarily learning activities; taking a 'coaching' stance (keeping inside leadership in charge of and owning the process while focusing on accelerating feedback); working from a development perspective (acknowledging that improvements are discovered as well as invented); and maintaining simultaneous focus on vision and its execution (seeking small wins as building blocks in a more continuous implementation effort). Coupled with a redefined process, the balanced scorecard promises to be a fruitful system indeed.[47]

Implementing your balanced scorecard

Avoiding common mistakes

The implementation process

Ongoing development of strategic performance measures

The shortest answer is doing. ENGLISH PROVERB

The person who is worthy of being a leader will never complain of the stupidity of his helpers, of the ingratitude of mankind, or of the inappreciation of the public.

ELBERT HUBBARD

Designing the vision statement, setting strategic objectives and choosing the right measures are important steps towards obtaining competitive advantage. A brilliantly designed scorecard counts for nothing if an organisation fails to implement it properly. Implementation has to be ongoing to effectively put the strategies to work. Chapter 9, Designing Your Balanced Scorecard, addressed the *what* and *why* of designing a scorecard. This chapter considers the *who, where* and *how*. Implementation is not an easy road; it is easier to develop strategies than to carry them out. Frequently, organisations encounter problems during the implementation phase.

AVOIDING COMMON MISTAKES

Why do organisations have trouble implementing their objectives? A number of potential factors can cause implementation problems.

Resistance to change

An organisation's current operations are designed to implement old plans and strategies. New strategies requiring new organisational patterns and behaviours may be resisted. The greater the disparity between the old and the new strategies, the greater the potential for resistance.

Over-emphasising short- or long-term goals

Strategic plans typically address *long-term* activities for the next three to five years. But the managers who implement these goals are rewarded on the basis of *short-term* results. Managers tend to favour short–term results compared with the long-term option: they have been conditioned to behave in this way. For example, when one organisation designed its internal business process objectives it stressed the importance of TQM. To increase quality, managers responded by reducing production levels and cutting staff when it could have retrained them. These managers met short-term performance goals and obtained good performance results, but their actions damaged the organisation's long-term strategy.

No detailed implementation plan

Some balanced scorecards are poorly implemented because the implementation team fails to make detailed implementation plans. Implementation teams may leave the detail to managers to work out and the result is either *poor* implementation or *no* implementation. The implementation team must prepare a detailed implementation plan that shows the specific activities needed to put the plan into action. This involves the preparation of detailed timetables and assigning major tasks to individual managers.

The planning process was ring fenced

This occurs when the scorecard has been designed by the organisation's leaders who may have little contact with middle and lower managers. A centrally based design phase is complemented because of the involvement of upper middle management in the process. Without this involvement, several problems can emerge. Senior managers are concerned with broad strategy and performance and can prepare measures that are too general. They may not understand the practical problems that are faced by line managers and may produce unrealistic measures. Or, lower middle managers who were not involved in designing the measures may not fully understand them and may resent what they consider to be unrealistic indicators of how the organisation is performing.

THE IMPLEMENTATION PROCESS

To implement the balanced scorecard, changes are potentially required to the ways hundreds of people make day-to-day decisions, internally and externally. This is not an overnight process, but should occur naturally, over time. The implementation team (frequently composed of the people who make up the Scorecard Design Team) must find ways to manage these actors.

1. The action plan

Managers work with other managers to obtain support for new initiatives. The finance manager might talk to the operations manager about production and inventory levels. They may then talk with human resources about employee matters and award variations. Marketing managers talk to clients, bankers and advertising agencies.

The action plan pulls all of these people and activities together in an organised manner by identifying the decisions and actions required to implement the objectives. It also passes accountability for these decisions and actions to specific people in the organisation. In turn, a time line of when action points must be completed is established. The action plan identifies when actions must be taken, who will make them and how decisions will be managed so that the organisation's objectives can be attained.

2. Organisational structure

In addition, an organisation's structure plays an integral role in the implementation of the strategies. The organisational structure can allow efficiency through specialisation. Separate roles can be linked by the structure and by setting lines of authority and communication.

In their study of successful companies, Peters and Waterman observed that many organisations had common structural characteristics that led to successful implementation.[48] For example, successful organisations tend to have more informal structures—Hewlett-Packard's MBWA (management by wandering around), IBM's 'open door' policy, and 3M's 'clubs' to create small group interaction. Successful organisational structures are decentralised, with small independent business units to encourage innovation. World-best organisations tend to have low employee levels. According to Peters and Waterman:

> *Indeed, it appears that most of our excellent companies have comparatively few people at the corporate level, and that what staff there is tends to be out in the field solving problems rather than in the home office checking on things. The bottom line is fewer administrators, more operators.*[49]

Some of Peters and Waterman's conclusions have been questioned because the study focused on high technology and consumer goods organisations operating in rapidly changing environments.[50]

3. Decision and compensation systems

Decision and compensation systems relate to internal policies that direct activities such as planning, information gathering, budgeting, recruiting and training, control, and personnel evaluation and rewards. Poorly designed balanced scorecard systems can work against implementation, compared with well-designed scorecards which assist implementation. This is clearly illustrated by compensation systems that emphasise the achievement of short-term objectives at the expense of long-term objectives.

4. Human resources

The scorecard is implemented by people. Accordingly, careful human resources planning is required. The organisation must have, at all levels, competent, cross-functional, motivated and capable people. Career succession planning and professional development planning are particularly important. With these, the organisation can link the appointment of managers to the needs of the strategic objectives.

Alfred P. Sloan Jr, said it best: 'take my assets but leave me my organisation and in 5 years I'll have it all back.'[51] The process of adapting to the new environment created by the balanced scorecard is served through holding a genuine appreciation for an organisation's real assets: its people. No bank account, internal policy or plant and equipment will determine the success or failure of the balanced scorecard. Ultimately, its success can be distilled down to one thing: the leaders of the organisation must demonstrate trust and respect for all staff, and must empower staff through their managers to execute the work of their role to the very best of their ability in accordance with the improvement initiatives and set targets.

Accordingly, an emphasis on voluntary staff participation may result in greater cooperation and a better system in the longer term. It takes longer than one might anticipate to develop measures that are understandable. Training needs should be incorporated in the process early on. Training which focuses on practical exercises in small group settings is recommended.

5. Organisation culture

An organisation's culture can make or break the implementation of a balanced scorecard. The term 'culture' in this instance refers to the beliefs and mythologies shared in the organisation. An organisation's culture indirectly guides the direction of an organisation. Whenever an organisation undergoes significant change, the leaders of an organisation must manage the culture so as not to send the wrong signals across the organisation. To illustrate, studies have shown that about three-quarters of international corporate mergers and acquisitions are 'disappointments or outright failures' simply because the acquiring company tends not to think much about integrating the culture of the two organisations. Accordingly, companies implementing the balanced scorecard need to work hard at addressing those all-important 'me' issues.[52]

6. Stay focused on the day-to-day business

In spite of everything going on inside your organisation, there is still a business to operate. Management cannot adopt the behaviour of a local bus company in Australia who, to keep in step with its timetable, had bus drivers simply driving past queues of waiting passengers. The leaders of the organisation cannot afford to be distracted by the implementation of the balanced scorecard.

7. Stay flexible

Stay flexible. A truly creative change process is by its very nature somewhat unpredictable. Solutions will emerge which were unanticipated at the outset. The effective change manager understands this and uses it to advantage by encouraging and embracing these new insights in the design of the balanced scorecard. The ability to see change as a continually unfolding process rather than simply the drive to implement a preordained solution can enable the effective leader to capitalise on, rather than resist, new views of the scorecard.

8. Stay focused on the client

The *process* of change should be invisible to clients, but the *results* of the implementation of the balanced scorecard should be apparent and positive. Reporting time frames relevant to different internal clients require careful attention. Shop-floor staff need assessment by direct supervision, probably on a daily basis, while at the higher management level it should be less often. The Network Operations business unit—the first Telstra Corporation Limited business unit to try the balanced scorecard—affirms this point.[53]

9. Software and systems

The IT systems environment may not, in its present state, easily deliver valuable balanced scorecard information. Significant development may be required. IT system upgrades or the purchase of new products can come with a high price tag. However, an organisation can still follow a logical migration path.

Fortunately, software vendors are beginning to recognise two distinct uses for software within a business context: systems which are primarily of a transaction-processing variety and those whose job it is to use this data for analysis. This is a useful way of looking at systems architecture and to provide more integrated solutions.

10. Clear internal communication lines

Communicating the facts means communicating all the relevant issues to the staff. It is necessary, therefore, to communicate:

- who will use the information and how;

- what benefits are being sought;

- how the new model will complement other improvement initiatives; and

- the potential impact (if any) on particular projects, planned capital expenditures and the associated processes which deliver client value.

That's exactly what Ericsson Australia has done. For this leading global tele-communications supplier, staff know where they stand and understand what the leaders are trying to implement. Since 1994, this company has done two checks on alignment of individual goals to company strategy and found in a sample size of 17% of staff that 94% of individual objectives were traceable to corporate objectives. There was a 75% alignment between the company's strategic objectives in 1995 and the business unit's objectives, and this improved to 85% in 1996. An Ericsson spokesperson has said it takes a lot of communication.[54]

How should the facts about the balanced scorecard be delivered across the organisation? Face-to-face. It is important to be clear about what 'face-to-face' means. For many organisations, face-to-face means large meetings with up to 30 employees, in many cases crammed into a room too small or with too few chairs. Such meetings fail in their ultimate objective; that is, they fail to comprehensively inform employees about the ways in which the balanced scorecard will affect the work of their roles today, tomorrow and the day after that. A survey by Larkin over 20 years across Canada, Australia, the United States and Britain has found that face-to-face communication is the most successful communication medium through which to convey a new order of things to employees. Face-to-face communication trumps communication by video at the rate of two to one![55]

If an employee foresees a potential role upheaval just around the corner, their logical reaction is to become fearful of the very thing (the change) they feel they are being pushed into. The tendency of people in such a circumstance is to fight—not out of a sense of conviction in the justness of one's cause, not out of confidence that they will win, but instinctively, because when one has unilateral change imposed on them, fighting is the normal thing to do.[56]

The line managers of all employees should advise them about the introduction of the balanced scorecard and how it will affect the work they do. The manager must build and maintain an effective team. Managers can objectively formulate and set the goals, targets and improvement plans for the employees in their teams in a manner concordant with the improvement initiatives conceived of during the design phase.[57]

You should empower your staff to take charge of the improvement initiatives that have been identified by them. For example, when Werner von Braun was in charge of the United States' Marshall Space Flight Centre (then headquarters of the nation's space program), any employee who noticed a defect in a piece of equipment was immediately put in command of a team to correct that defect. A mere private first class or G-3 (one of the lowest-ranking civilians in governmental employ) could be made the boss of company, or even field-grade officers.[58]

The competition to find defects was, in some respects, demoralising to senior members of the Centre. However, it also resulted in significantly higher quality control. Notably, communication and sponsorship includes the need to ensure that adequate top-level visibility, support and resourcing are given to the system in balance with, or in recognition of, the drivers to move forward.

It is also important to recognise:

▶ the scale of change required through the need to make progress;

▶ the availability of appropriate skills within the organisation to deliver such change; and

▶ the strategy for communication which best fits the cultural style of the organisation.

ONGOING DEVELOPMENT OF STRATEGIC PERFORMANCE MEASURES

The development of the balanced scorecard must be maintained over time. The establishment of a Strategic Review Committee can serve this purpose effectively. The Committee acts as a control mechanism to review the effectiveness of the new system, to identify improvement opportunities and system improvements. In this way, the Committee can recommend ongoing and comprehensive strategic system reviews, with an emphasis on involving all divisions of the organisation in the process—including the various stakeholders such as the supervisors and shop-floor staff, clients, suppliers and substantial shareholders.

The composition of the Committee should mirror the leadership and interest in the balanced scorecard. Outward demonstration of senior-level commitment can help to maintain impetus as the organisation is redefined by its competitive environment.

SUMMARY

Balanced scorecard techniques are in widespread use, and strategic performance measurement is here to stay. Despite the reasons supporting a scorecard system, there still exists a very real danger that the full benefits of the balanced scorecard may not be realised due to a lack of an integrated implementation approach. However, the scorecard's use in a number of the world-class organisations, like Mobil Oil, is now taking root. Genuine balanced scorecard implementation is a complex and long-term undertaking. Therefore, before any organisation sets off along this path, it should consider carefully three pre-conditions for success: the organisation will need to understand *who* is accountable for implementing the new performance management system; *where* the organisation wants to be (and to be convinced of the benefits to be gained once it succeeds); and *how* the organisation intends to get there.

Sometimes these pre-conditions are not satisfied and the organisation, as a whole, cannot see why a scorecard methodology should be introduced, how it can be implemented or what the real and potential benefits are from implementation. In these cases, the organisation may need to take a pilot-program approach until it becomes clear how these pre-conditions can be met. Taking this approach, most organisations become convinced of the value of moving to full-scale integration.

Benchmarking your performance measures

Why benchmark?

What is benchmarking?

The benchmarking process

Avoiding common mistakes

If you know your enemy and know yourself, you need not fear the result of a hundred battles. SUN TZU, THE ART OF WAR, 500 B.C.

Benchmarking aligns perfectly with Sun Tzu's view in that it is critical for world-class organisations to evaluate the four dimensions of their business (client, financial, internal processes, and learning and growth) from an *external* perspective.

A vital step in designing your balanced scorecard system is establishing goals that you have a reasonable chance of attaining. Benchmarking is a consideration that can help you to set goals, targets and improvement initiatives by informing you of your competitor's performance. Accordingly, this chapter considers the steps required for a successful benchmarking effort, the role of leadership in effectively *launching* and *maintaining* such an initiative, and how to side-step common mistakes.

WHY BENCHMARK?

Strategic planning is now a widely-practised and well-documented technique, and has helped many organisations address questions like:

▶ What market segments for products and services appear to offer the most potential?

▶ How will these market segments evolve over time?

▶ What are the critical success factors required to serve each market segment effectively?

▶ What are the strategies, strengths, weaknesses, opportunities and threats of my competitors?

▶ How do my competitors' core capabilities map against the strategic objectives for the four dimensions of the balanced scorecard for a segment?

Addressing these questions has allowed a number of organisations to develop *innovative goals*. However, even the most brilliant deployment plan will fail unless it is implemented successfully. That is why many organisations continue to exhibit slow or no growth when more aggressive competitors increase their share of the market. There are three main reasons underpinning an organisation's decision to benchmark.

1. Improve client satisfaction

Benchmarking is an additional tool in your toolkit to help you establish at a generic level what is important to clients. Your clients are concerned with *time*, *performance and service*, and *price*. Industry best practices demonstrate what is important to clients. Goals can be tailored to improve client satisfaction.

2. Establish targets and improvement initiatives

Benchmarking is a credible target-setting technique because it relies on industry best practices as the basis for setting your targets. In turn, the targets become the yardstick by which managers can determine their improvement plans. It drives the pursuit of an organisation's strategic objectives through the alignment of people's behaviour to industry best practice. The improvement plan—which specifically incorporates the benchmarked targets—injects a vital extra dimension into the way people approach the work of their roles.

3. Drive continuous improvement

Benchmarking can increase an organisation's level of self-awareness by asking the question: what should we excel at in order to achieve that target? Armed with vital information concerning the way in which the industry leader excels at the process should stimulate new ways of thinking about processes, and even productive variations of best practice to further enhance your organisation's performance.

WHAT IS BENCHMARKING?

Benchmarking is not *comparative analysis*, where an analyst looks at how the organisation compares with others in terms of measures like the sales per employee, productivity per machine, cost per unit, overhead rates or growth in market share. Those measures do not drive change and do not specifically focus on the processes which can create superior performance.

Process re-engineering is not a form of benchmarking either. Process re-engineering describes the process of evaluating internal processes then making improvements by applying a variety of techniques. For example, an organisation wants to improve the administration of its corporate credit card system, so it looks at the system then *inwardly* works on process steps to improve the performance of the system.

A *survey* is not the same as a benchmarking study. Some organisations gather information via client surveys about inefficiencies clients perceive to exist in the practices and processes of the organisation and suggested ways to go about improving them. The information gathering process of a survey is fundamentally different to a benchmarking project.

In addition, benchmarking studies have *partners*. Surveys only have participants. A semantic difference you say? Not so. A survey participant is usually selected on the basis of the degree of *likeness* to the organisation (e.g. common geographic area, type of client base) and may frequently request anonymity. A benchmarking partner, on the other hand, expects to learn something in return for sharing information about its own organisation. Moreover, the output of a benchmarking partner may differ significantly from your own. Generally, surveys report aggregated and averaged information from numerous participants to protect the identity of the interviewees. Benchmark output *may* include this type of information, but most often it will detail best practices for the process or function under investigation.

Many managers completely miss the point of benchmarking. Benchmarking is not an easily-accomplished once-off effort. In particular, it is not a three-hour 'look and see' session with another organisation where they tell you what they are doing and you say, 'That's a good idea. We will do the same!' You then return with one or two ideas and try to make a change. In that type of situation, no improvement mechanism has been developed, nor has a clear pathway been pioneered for future improvement. Nor have any measurements of success typically been put in place. The object of benchmarking, therefore, is to institutionalise the improvement ethic.[59]

Put simply, benchmarking is a systematic approach to creating and driving change into an organisation. Change is created by doing process-to-process (or function-to-function) comparisons with other organisations and by developing detailed information about performance levels and practices. In other words, benchmarking is the search for industry best practices that lead to competitive advantage.[60] If you are considering doing a benchmarking study to establish your goals and targets for your scorecard, then you must ask three primary questions:

1. *Where are we now?* Too frequently, organisations become complacent about objectively evaluating their effectiveness and efficiency. Most organisations have an intuitive sense of how well their processes or functions are operating. What is commonly missing however, is an in-depth understanding of cost, quality and response-time performance.

2. *Where do we want to be?* When comparing your organisation with competitors, you may find that one or more of your benchmarking partners can demonstrate significantly better bottom-line results than yourself.

3. *How do we get there?* Simply knowing that someone else is much better than you is the first step down the road to best practice. The trick is to determine how similar performance levels can be achieved in your own organisation. What practices do you need to adopt to be as good as the best?

You can make real gains from 'borrowing' ideas. The wine industry in the United States—like that in other countries—used to consist of a myriad of small, independent vineyards, selling wine to a relatively small customer base through specialist distribution channels. There was little consumer branding. Companies like Gallo reasoned that instead of being an elitist product sold to connoisseurs, wine could reach a far larger market if it were treated like fast-moving customer goods, reaping economies in production, distribution and marketing. They changed the face of their industry and expanded the market enormously.[61]

As a fundamental change management tool, benchmarking studies broaden the horizons of your managers and staff by helping them realise that 'there can be a better way'. A successful benchmarker sheds the 'not invented here' syndrome by eliminating such mythologies as 'others cannot teach us anything'. A new philosophy can emerge characterised by beliefs like 'We can learn from others'. It can be far easier to convince staff that the best practice way *is* achievable and not another theoretical possibility if you can point to somebody else already doing it who is making it work. You are also saved the effort of reinventing the wheel.[62]

THE BENCHMARKING PROCESS

Why does benchmarking fail for so many organisations? A birds-eye conspectus of the generic benchmarking process is straightforward. Look at Table 18 for an illustration of the steps involved. Successful implementation of this process is nevertheless something of a mystery. In the next section, we will demystify the subject for you.

TABLE 18

The benchmarking process

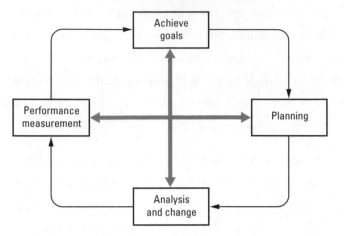

1. Scope the project

What do you expect benchmarking to accomplish and why? Optimally, your benchmarking study should focus on the issues most important to your clients (internal and external) and/or which may have the most opportunity for improvement so that your targets and improvement initiatives can be tailored accordingly.

Build support for the benchmarking study at the beginning of the bench-marking design process. One member of the Scorecard Design Team could be appointed to coordinate the study. As a successful benchmarker therefore, you should focus your initiatives on important issues where the users are committed to achieving results. Many organisations new to benchmarking have missed this point. Some have tried to benchmark virtually every process. In contrast, some organisations prefer to address those areas which are simple to understand and measure, or those which are secondary but will serve as a good first try. The likely outcome in either case is that significant time and money will be expended with little material impact on the bottom line. As an example, assume that three areas in your organisation merit the most potential for improvement:

▶ Various managers feel that the responsiveness of information technology personnel to their requests is too slow.

▶ Despite the large investment in a new computer software package, administration costs are still excessive. The technology has not delivered a net positive return.

▶ Despite every effort by your organisation, employee morale is still too low.

On which area should your focus lie? Resist all temptations to address any of these areas unless they are truly important and until you have the support of key leaders. Similarly, if you pursue the 'easiest' option of the group, it probably means that you lack the resources and competency to deal with the hard issues.

2. Define your benchmarking approach

The ultimate success of your benchmarking program depends to a large extent on the conceptual soundness of your benchmarking approach. The next section outlines one approach which should place you in good stead.

Partner selection

At some point early on in the benchmarking study it is necessary to select one or more benchmarking partners. Ask the question: which organisation has the best industry practices against which we can benchmark? That question is answered not merely by selecting the industry leader, or settling on a competitor of whom the greatest amount of information exists, although both of these factors are relevant. The critical factor in determining a benchmarking partner is to select a competitor (which has a comparative advantage over your organisation) whose business, functions and processes are similar to your own. In other words, the performance drivers should be the same. Depending on the type of business that your organisation carries out, selection of a partner could be difficult; many differences exist between all organisations; for example, organisational structure, size, level of turnover.

Striving to be a world-class organisation can cause some organisations to do too much too soon. It would suffice for most to adopt a more gradual strategy. Trying to immediately mirror what a world-class organisation is doing would be like giving a learner driver a Formula 1 car to practise in. Your organisation may not yet be ready to implement the power of these practices. Remember that your goals, targets and improvement plans must be realistically attainable.

Provided that a competitor is selected for whom many of the processes are the same, the selection process should be relatively easy to conclude. For areas of your business which are unmatched, but for which performance must be tracked because they are critical areas of the organisation (and therefore require goals etc) simply select other partners whose processes are the same *in these areas*.

To illustrate, Fruity Bell (not its real name), a successful manufacturer and wholesaler of ice-cream, needed to determine its benchmarking partner as part of the target-setting process of implementing a balanced scorecard in 1996. Fruity Bell, an Australian company, sells most of its ice-cream overseas, although some is sold locally. It was easy to select the prime benchmarking partner. It happened to be a New Zealand ice-cream wholesaler of similar size and maturity, and which used similar processes at the manufacturing plant. But one significant difference existed—the New Zealand wholesaler sold all of its ice-cream locally. Fruity Bell searched and found a secondary partner specialising in the export of ice-cream to benchmark its selling processes.

Benchmarking approaches

There are at least four types of benchmarking that can be performed to help an organisation finely tune its goals and targets:

▶ Competitive benchmarking.

▶ Functional benchmarking.

▶ Internal benchmarking.

▶ Generic benchmarking.

Competitive benchmarking

Same-product competitors are the most obvious choice against which to bench-mark. Often the largest drawback is the size of operations. If the competitor is too big or too small, then it makes your task of obtaining meaningful comparisons more difficult, and in some cases even valueless. An example could be Fruity Bell and the New Zealand manufacturer. Any meaningful comparison on domestic delivery costs would need to take into account the *size* and *frequency* of shipments, ability to negotiate with freight carriers, whether containers are owned or rented, proximity to the railhead, wharves and so on.

Functional benchmarking

Functional benchmarking attempts to overcome the weaknesses inherent in competitive benchmarking on the basis that it is not necessary to benchmark against same-product competitors. This approach is valuable for identifying functional competitors with best practices to benchmark who may operate in different industries to you. This would involve, in the case of domestic delivery charges, identifying Australian export companies who are perceived to have superior delivery systems.

A decision to use functional benchmarking would depend on your ability to identify functional leaders from other industries who have similar *client-oriented objectives*. For example, the physical dimensions of the products must not be dissimilar: size, weight, mode of shipment must all facilitate meaningful analysis. Determining the leading functional competitors can be easy. Software vendors are a valuable sources of information here. They would be likely to divulge their clients—even promote the more famous ones.

Internal benchmarking

For larger organisations, often the easiest way to conduct benchmarking investigations is to compare internal business processes. That may involve a comparison of delivery charges between different divisions or business units. Information and its collection should be readily available and the problem of commercial sensitivity of information may not arise. The benchmarking effort can be as thorough and complete as you like. No information gaps need exist.

Generic benchmarking

You may decide that generic benchmarking is the way forward. Some internal business processes are the same, no matter in which industry an organisation operates (e.g. receivables collection). The attraction of generic benchmarking is that best practices and processes can be identified from any industry. Proven practices may be re-engineered with only minor adjustment.

3. Understand the benchmarking process

By and large, the main benefit of benchmarking derives from the required analysis of your organisation's own operations. Many leaders do not have a precise handle on how well certain processes are functioning. Considered below are key issues to be aware of whenever you undertake a benchmarking effort.

Accurate information

The importance of accurate information must be stressed. Why would you want to adopt another organisation's practices if its processes do not perform as well as yours? In particular, be clear on understanding what is included in the unit cost measures: costs can look radically different depending on what another organisation has included in the measure. For example, absorbed costs—typically administration, occupancy charges, and information technology—are best excluded initially. So too should-payroll related costs, such as health insurance and payroll tax, be excluded. It is a cost/effectiveness trade-off. Your information about the benchmarking partner can be sourced internally from the organisation, and externally from information which is in the public domain. See Table 19 below for a comprehensive list of these.

Use of the internet

The use of the internet has also become a valuable tool to collect, capture and share information from different sources. The internet provides many capabilities, including the capability to transfer data files electronically. Large amounts of data can be transferred from one location to another in a matter of seconds. This capability can improve the timeliness of obtaining information necessary to support organisational performance measurement analyses.

Treatment of 'outliers'

In constructing control charts (i.e. charts which compare the performance of your operation with the performance of your competitor's operations), individual or groups of data points may appear near or beyond the calculated control limit lines. Since this information appears to indicate that a system is or may not be in control (e.g. stable), additional evaluation may be needed to ascertain if the data in question are the result of common cause or special cause variation. If the data are clearly influenced by a one-time aberration (e.g. special cause), there could be a basis for

TABLE 19   **Sources of information for benchmarking study**

Internal	External
Libraries	Trade and professional associations
Databases	Industry publications
Inhouse reviews	Relevant journals
Inhouse periodicals	Industry databases
	Industry experts
	University publications
	University libraries
	Patents office
	Media releases
	Company financial reports
	Consulting firms
	Personal networks

excluding the number or estimating what the actual value should have been for the purpose of determining actual system control limits.

Process capability

Process capability is a determination of whether an existing process is capable of attaining the specified (or desired) performance. Naturally, the goals, targets and improvement initatives which you ultimately decide on must be realistic enough that the underlying processes are capable of achieving them. Process capability has a precise, limited definition in a manufacturing context. This determination is based upon observing the history of the process output data. Statistical process control is used to determine the expected bounds of the data. These bounds (which are the three standard deviation control limits) are compared with the manufacturing specification for the process.

Management philosophy

Use of statistical process control with performance indicator data provides important information for managers. Managers can use the process capability information in order to manage the processes they are responsible for. The control limits provide a reasonable guarantee of the expected extreme values of the process data. If these extreme values (and/or the average) are determined to be unacceptable, then management must embark on process changes in order to improve the outcome of the process.

Many management philosophies focus upon outcomes. There is justification in this, as it can be said that without the bottom-line outcomes, an organisation will not stay in business. However, it must be realised that outcomes are the result of processes. In order to improve on existing outcomes, the process that created the outcomes in question must be understood and management must create changes to these processes.

Accordingly, managers must understand the processes that they control. In order to improve, the existing process capability must be known. Statistical process control and process capability provide the tools to:

▶ Measure current performance.
▶ Describe the state of statistical control.
▶ Attain statistical control.

▶ Determine if process changes are needed.

▶ Determine the effects of process changes once implemented.

The relativity matrix

You need to be able to obtain a credible comparison. Incompatible benchmarking partners should have been eliminated earlier on. Highly competent business analysts can adjust for any anomalies between you and your benchmarking partner so that comparisons can still be meaningful. Anomalies, in this context, refers to factors which, on their face value, would appear to preclude any meaningful comparisons being made. In the previous example, the overhead costs of the New Zealand ice-cream manufacturer were materially less than the overhead costs of Fruity Bell. The reason of course, was due to the differing rental payments each made because the geographic location of each of their manufacturing plants was different. Rational adjustments to the information can maintain 'like and like'.

It is also important to hold on to the reigns tightly when it comes to verifying the integrity of the information that your benchmarking partner has supplied. Information errors and misinterpretation among benchmarkers are all too common.

4. Identify performance gaps and best practices

What factors explain the gap between one organisation and the industry's best? Superior performance can be highly visible in overhead costs (e.g. cost of premises) and in the information technology (e.g. the software packages used). But in many instances, the factors giving the partner a competitive advantage are more difficult to identify, such as management practices, employee remuneration systems, culture, leadership or the right mix of people. Often the task of quantifying factors like these is a difficult process and a time-consuming one too.

5. Devise and implement targets and improvement initiatives

Your newly designed, top-level balanced scorecard requires meaningful goals and targets. To achieve these goals and targets, an action plan will be necessary. An action plan assigns improvement initiatives to managers based on the results of your benchmarking study. Speaking generally, the failure of benchmarking efforts to produce tangible results is often tied to the magnitude of organisational change required to achieve the requisite impact. Many leaders simply do not appreciate the extent of change necessary to transform behaviour across the organisation.

Even though benchmarking studies are a straightforward process when done properly, six critical mistakes are typically made by an organisation attempting this technique for the first time.

No support from leaders

Successful benchmarking exercises must be visibly embraced by your leaders. For some reason, many exercises have their genesis at a lower layer in the organisation—with marginal, if any, support from the top. There is every reason for making the organisation's leaders aware of the benchmarking project and supporting it. Moreover, their ebullience must reach all employees throughout the organisation, along with clear objectives and the expressed need to shed the 'not invented here' syndrome. This may not arise as an issue for smaller businesses, but in organisations where not every employee sees the leader on a day-to-day basis, the need for top-level commitment becomes necessary.

Poor team selection

The cross-functional nature of most processes today typifies the need to hand pick teams of the right members. Unfortunately, the following circumstance is all too common: the message emanates from the top that your organisation will be commencing its first benchmarking study as part of the balanced scorecard design process in a month or so, and you need to nominate one of your own subordinates to participate. 'Terrific' you say, 'Another drain on my already depleted person power'. So, what do you do? You *will* assign someone—but it's hardly likely to be one of your best people.

Too frequently the staff who are selected are simply those available at the time. That problem is then compounded by poor preparation and orientation of the benchmarkers in such fundamental areas as: W*hat* is benchmarking? *Why* do you need to do it? *How* does it work? *What* are the objectives? Hence, the need for training. Training is not rocket science, nor is it a quick-skim-the-surface four-hour exercise. Thinking in benchmarking terms is different from what most people are used to, which usually necessitates a longer time frame for concepts to 'sink in'.

Accordingly, if the Scorecard Design Team will also manage the benchmarking study, it is vital that the members represent an appropriate blend of operational capability and expertise. It requires a certain level of expertise to recognise a 'best practice' in another organisation. Benchmarkers need internal credibility also. Their recommendations which flow from their investigations are likely to challenge ideas which are deeply ingrained into the organisation. Some resistance is to be expected. This resistance can best be overcome if the change agents command respect on site. Even if the project has the support of the senior managers and the right team, the project will still fail if it is not supported continually.

Project objectives are ambiguous

Be clear about the outcomes the benchmarking project is intended to produce. The scope of the undertaking also needs to be skillfully managed. Your initial thoughts about what to study may be much too ambitious. Wanting to benchmark the client satisfaction, internal business processes and employee development indicators of your partner is the same as tackling the drought problem. If done correctly—with the right team, the right benchmarking partners, enough financial backing, and in-depth analysis of information—it will take you forever. Instead, benchmarking the logistics of the product delivery process because of suspected major opportunities is much more manageable.

Unrealistic time and cost expectations

The timing of benchmarking projects relative to the budgeting cycle is important. If well timed, results can be easily built into next year's plan. It is unrealistic to see a 2–3 month deadline put on benchmarking studies; 4–6 months is about the minimum that can be expected to yield good results—and that is for an organisation that is experienced at benchmarking. Projects which take longer than 12 months may suffer because the benchmarking partners begin to lose interest. In juxtaposition, project cost is frequently underestimated.

Poor understanding of information

Benchmarkers who have not done their research—who are not 100% sure of what their objectives are—are frequently guilty of getting caught up in the numbers game. If you can measure it, you can manage it and if you can manage it, you can improve it. But numbers are simply indicators of processes and practices which are working well. The goal is to understand what is behind the numbers.

Poor implementation of change

Fundamentally, benchmarking is about change. So why devote all that effort just to let the results gather dust on a shelf? Frequently it is because the organisation is not ready for the opportunities brought to light.

SUMMARY

An organisation setting out to establish its goals, targets and improvement initiatives through benchmarking must be ready for major change. Benchmarking can uncover the need for revamped reporting relationships, for organisation-wide change, for new remuneration systems, improved employee productivity and many other things besides. If your organisation is not up to this kind of overhaul, following through with a 'half-hearted' or non-existent effort will very quickly lead to a nil return on the benchmarking investment you have made.

CONCLUSION

I hope that you now ask yourself the question 'How can I measure performance?' more frequently than before you read this book. Measuring performance is not easy, but the process is simplified by using the conceptually based approach that I have described. Your organisation can now obtain the results you want.

The solution is to follow the path to success that a disciplined approach to performance measurement can provide. The balanced scorecard system meets that criteria. If this book has enabled you to evaluate your current performance measurement programs and perhaps you can see that your systems require renovation to provide you with greater focus, then hopefully you now have the skills to implement change.

My main objectives in writing this book were:

1. to explain the conceptual grounding of the balanced scorecard performance measurement framework;
2. to work through the balanced scorecard design and implementation process and to explore their implications; and
3. to consider how the balanced scorecard approach applies to a wide variety of management situations and strategic change issues across all types of organisations.

The balanced scorecard concept has traditionally been a tool for use by executives and managers of multinational firms. In my opinion the concept has a much broader application. Accordingly, one of my goals of writing this book has been to demystify the concept so that the business entrepreneur, small business proprietors, service providers (e.g. lawyers, accountants and medical practitioners) and employees alike can implement the model.

It is useful to think of *Future Success* as a three-part solution. First, I have explained *why* organisations require a new order of measuring and managing performance. Then I challenged you to understand *what* the balanced scorecard can do for your organisation to help it achieve a competitive edge in the marketplace. Finally, you now have the knowledge of *how* to integrate design with implementation as the system unfolds in the competitive environment. Need, design, implementation and integration can now come together so that your organisation can realise its full strategic potential.

Through the concepts, principles, experiences and examples used in this book, you can implement the balanced scorecard in your own organisation.

Sample performance measures

This appendix is included to stimulate your thinking about appropriate measures. However, remember that the measures you select should be tailored to the processes, products and services, and goals of the organisation.

Accounting performance measurements

Percentage of errors in reports

Errors reported by outside auditors

Numbers of complaints by users

Amount of time spent…

Appraising/correcting input errors

Length of time to prepare and send a
bill

Number of final accounting jobs rerun

Amount of intra-company accounting
bill-back activity

Number of open items

Percentage of advances outstanding

Percentage of data entry errors in
accounts payable and general
ledger

Percentage of shipments requiring
more than one attempt to invoice

Average number of days from receipt to
processing

Percentage of late reports

Errors in input to Information
Technology

Percentage of input errors detected

Number of hours per week correcting
or number of complaints about
changing documents
inefficiencies or excessive paper

Payroll processing time

Percentage of errors in payroll

Age of debtors

Number of equipment sales miscoded

Time spent correcting erroneous inputs

Percentage of deviations from cash plan

Time to process travel expense accounts

Machine billing turnaround time

Credit approval turnaround time

Number of untimely supplier invoices
processed

Clerical performance measurements

Misfiles per week

Administration errors (using the
wrong procedure)

Percentage of action items not done
on schedule

Percentage of coding errors on time
cards

Percentage of phone calls answered
within two rings

Pages processed error-free per hour

Percentage of work retyped

Number of errors per page

Number of times messages are not
delivered

Percentage of inputs not received on
schedule

Period reports not completed on
schedule

Percentage of phone calls dialed
correctly

Clerical personnel/personnel support

Product/development engineering performance measurements

Percentage of designs released on schedule

Number of times a design is changed

Design accuracy

Rate of client satisfaction with design

Percentage of error-free designs

Percentage of problems solved first time

Time required to make an engineering change

Percentage of data recording errors per month

Percentage on quotations which are successful

Number of meetings held per quarter

Cycle time to correct client problem

Number of products that pass independent evaluation error-free

Number of unsuccessful pre-analyses

Percentage of requests for engineering action open for more than two weeks

Number of restarts and tests

Number of days for the release cycle

Percentage of bills of material that are released in error

Cost of engineering changes per month

Client cost per life of output delivered

Percentage of drafting errors per design

Percentage of errors in cost estimates

Number of off-specifications approved

Accuracy of advance materials list

Field performance of product

Percentage of errors found during design review

Time to correct a problem

Percentage of reports with errors in them

Percentage of evaluations that meet engineering objectives

Percentage of test plans that are changed (change/test plan) where quality and defect prevention were the main subject

Number of problems that were also encountered in previous products

Number of errors in publications reported from the plan and field

Number of misused shipments of prototypes

Number of off-specifications accepted

Number of days late to pre-analysis

Effectiveness of regression tests

Percentage of corrective action schedules missed

Cost of input errors to the computer

Spare parts cost after warranty

Financial performance measurements

Percentage error in budget predictions

Percentage of financial reports delivered on schedule

Percentage of error-free invoices sent to clients

Percentage of errors in accounts payable

Number of payroll errors per month

Number of errors in financial reports

Percentage of errors in expense
    accounts

Net assets to sales

Current (quick) assets to current
    liabilities

Average age of receivables

Activity based costing

Age of inventory

Debt to equity ratio

Return on total assets

Gross profit

Share price analysis

Internal rate of return on assets

Earnings per share

Contribution margin per unit

Cash flow analysis

Sales growth

Economic value added

Computer rerun time due to input errors

Number of recorded errors per

employee

Percentage of bills paid so organisation
    gets price break

Number of entry errors per week

Number of errors found by outside
    auditors

Percentage of errors in travel advance
    records

Debtors to total current assets

Receivables turnover

Average inventory

Product costs

Interest coverage measure

Return on investment

Return on equity

Contrubution per employee

Sales per employee

Cost of capital

Price/earnings ratio

Life cycle cost

Inventory turnover

Price per unit

Industrial/plant engineering performance measurements

Percentage of manufacturing time lost
    due to unplanned downtime

Percentage of error in purchase orders

Scrap and rework due to calibration
    errors

Changes to planned downtime

Percentage variation to cost estimates

Percentage of equipment maintained
    on schedule

Accuracy of assets report

Number of industrial design

completions past due

Number of errors found after
    construction had been accepted
    by the organisation

Maintenance cost/equipment cost

Percentage of facilities on schedule

Percentage of error in time estimates

Hours lost due to plant downtime

Repeat call hours for the same problem

Percentage deviation from budget

Number of unscheduled maintenance

calls

Number of hours expended on
scheduled maintenance

Percentage of plant overdue for
calibration

Percentage of total floor space devoted

to storage

Number of mechanical/functional
errors in industrial design artwork

Percentage of engineering action
requests accepted

Forecasting performance measurements

Number of project plans that meet
schedule, price, and quality

Percentage of forecasting assumption
errors

Cost of producing forecast results

Cost of reviewing forecast results

Number of upward cost revisions per
year

Percentage error in sales forecasts

Number of changes in product
schedules

Cost of auditing forecast results

Information systems performance measurements

Keypunch errors per day

Reruns caused by operator error

Errors per thousand lines of code

Percentage of time required to debug
programs

Percentage error in forecast

Percentage of coding errors found
during formal testing

Percentage of test case runs before success

Percentage of documentation errors

Percentage of errors found after formal
test

Percentage of process step errors
before a correct package is ready

Percentage of changes to customer
requirements

Percentage of client problems not
corrected per schedule

Percentage change in client satisfaction

System availability

Rework costs resulting from computer
program

Time before help calls are answered

Input correction on data entry

Percentage of reports delivered on
schedule

Number of changes after the program
is coded

Number of cost estimates revised

Percentage error inlines of code
required

Percentage of test case errors

Percentage of revisions to plan

Percentage of revisions to program
objectives

Percentage of error-free programs
delivered to client

Percentage of revisions to checkpoint
plan

Percentage of programs not flow–

diagrammed

Percentage of problems uncovered
    before design release

Legal performance measurements

Response time on request for legal
    opinion

Number of solicitors per partner

Average number of hours recorded per
    lawyer but not billed

Average number of drafts to finalise
    agreements

Percentage of legal work undertaken
    inside budget

Average period of employment of
    lawyers

Lawyer turnover rates

Time to partner

Percentage of new business to old
    business

Percentage of earnings derived from
    top clients

Number of paralegals per lawyer

Number of secretaries per lawyer

Percentage of lawyers who can speak,
    read and write two or more
    languages fluently

Percentage of new work generated by
    referral

Percentage of tenders lodged being
    successful

Percentage of cases lost

Age of client relationship

Market share

Percentage of defect-free artwork

Terminal response time

Mean time between system repairs

Client satisfaction

Client loyalty

Age of debtors

Number of complaints from clients

Percentage of client complaints
    resolved first time

Average increase in hourly rates of
    lawyers

Lawyer and secretary absenteeism rates

Percentage of successful law suits

Percentage of law suits successfully
    defended

Percentage of their legal work a client
    gives your law firm

Percentage of legal bill to plaintiff's
    total award of damages

Percentage of lawyers using portable
    computers

Average number of hours billed per
    lawyer

Average number of hours spent in
    current legal education per
    lawyer

Average number of hours billed by
    lawyers but subsequently written
    off

Time to prepare patent claims

Average size of client accounts

$ spent on training per employee

Management performance measurements

Intellectual property violations per year

Percentage of targets missed

Percentage decrease in output per employee

Percentage error in planning estimates

Percentage of employees not promoted to new roles

Percentage of meetings that do not start on schedule

Number of role improvement ideas per employee

Change in market share

Percentage of performance appraisals done on schedule

Percentage of unsatisfactory appraisal results

Number of employee grievances per month

Percentage of employees active in professional societies

Percentage of employees late per month

Percentage of documents that require rework

Percentage of employee suggestions not implemented

Number of decisions initiated by lower-level management

Percentage of employees studying extracurricularly

Percentage of employees not finishing outside courses

Improvement in customer satisfaction survey

Revenue actual versus plan

Number of procedures with fewer than three acronyms and abbreviations

Percentage of employees active in improvement teams

Number of user complaints per month

Percentage revenue/expense ratio below plan

Percentage of departments with disaster recovery plans

Percentage of employees with development direct/indirect ratio plans

Number of iterations of strategic plan

Dollars saved per employee due to new ideas and/or methods

Number of tasks for which actual time exceeded estimated time

Warranty costs

Percentage variation of cost centres from budget

Employee turnover rate

Absenteeism rate

Percentage of output delivered on schedule and right first time

Business unit morale index

Percentage of employee time spent planning tasks

Ratio of full-time employees to contractors

Return on investment

Percentage of changes to project equipment required

Percentage of employee output that is
not measured

Number of training sessions conducted
per month

Percentage of employees active in
community activities

Percentage of time program plans are
met

Percentage of employees who can
detect and fix their own errors

Improvement in opinion surveys

Percentage of time cards that have errors
on them signed by managers

Percentage of meetings cancelled by the
meeting organiser

Ratio of part-time to full-time
employees

Volume actual versus planned

Percentage of policies less than two
pages

Number of formal reviews before plans
are approved

Number of hours per year of career and
skill development training per full-
time employee

Average time spent in one role per
employee

Percentage of executive interviews with
employees

Percentage of appraisals with quality as a
line item that makes up more than
50 % of the evaluation

Sales generated over period of time

Number of employees participating in
cost reduction programes

Peer evaluation reviews

Data integrity surveys

Cost of poor quality

Manufacturing performance measurements

Percentage of tools that pass minimum
legal requirements

Number of process changes per
operation due to error

Time required to solve a problem

Percentage error in test equipment
and tooling budget

Percentage of errors caused by
inadequate training

Activity based costing

Percentage of experiments that need
to be revised

Percentage of plant ready for
production on schedule

Percentage of drafting errors found by
auditors

Percentage of product that goes
through quality control processes

Percentage correlation between unplanned downtime and late orders

Fuel economy rates per machine

Number of hours expended to design
tools

Return on production assets

Annual cost of running machines

Number of process improvements
suggested per employee per
annum

Unplanned downtime index

Percentage error in manufacturing
   costs

Length of delays because process
   instructions are wrong or not
   available

Number of errors in operator training
   documentation

Percentage of employees not certified

Percentage error in output product
   quality

Value of stock unaccounted for by
stocktake

Average response time of repair
   companies

Average maintenance cost per
   machine

Annual budget on maintenance costs

Annual costs allocated to new
   machines

Electricity and gas machine running
   costs

Equipment utilisation

Number of accidents per month

Production control performance measurements

Percentage of products exceeding shelf
   life

Time required to incorporate
   engineering changes

Percentage of products that meet client
   orders

Time that line is down due to
   materials shortage

Annual increase or decrease of
   materials costs

Percentage of stock errors

Number of bill of lading errors not
   caught in shipping department

Cost of inventory spoilage and wastage

Percentage of errors in stocking

Percentage of manufacturing jobs
   completed on schedule

Percentage of errors in purchase orders

Inventory turnover rate

Percentage of time parts are not in
   stock when ordered from parts
   supplier

Spare parts availability

Age of inventory

Cost of unplanned shipments

Quality assurance performance measurements

Percentage error in reliability
   projections

Time to answer client complaints

Percentage of client complaints
   resolved at first point of call

Number of audits performed on
   schedule

Percentage of quality controls per
   overview-in-process

Percentage of engineering changes
   after design review

Number of errors in reports

Percentage of suppliers at 100% lot
   acceptance per year

Percentage of problems identified in the field

Percentage of reports published on schedule

Percentage of field returns correctly analysed

Percentage of IT services not completed on schedule

Percentage of errors in defect records

Number of client calls to report errors

Percentage of correlated test results with suppliers

Number of requests for corrective action being processed

Number of off-specifications approved

Number of manufacturing interruptions caused by supplier parts

Percentage product cost related to appraisal

Percentage of qualified suppliers

Cost of scrap and rework that was not created at the rejected operation

Percentage of products that meets client expectations

Cost of client complaints

Percentage of employees active in professional societies

Percentage of quality assurance personnel to total personnel

Percentage of management

Security/safety performance measurements

Time to get clearance

Percentage of documents classified incorrectly

accountants to product and manufacturing employees

Number of process changes after process qualification

Time to correct a problem

Percentage of products going directly to stock

Variations between inspectors performing the same role

Number of complaints from manufacturing management

Time to identify and solve problems

Percentage of improvement in early detection of major design errors

Number of reject orders not resolved in three days

Percentage of committed supplier plans in place

Inspection cycle time

Time required to process a request for corrective action

Percentage of part numbers going directly to stock

Percentage error in predicting customer performance

Percentage skip lot inspection scrap and rework

Number of problems identified in-process

Percentage of audits conducted on schedule

Number of safety problems identified

vs number of problems rectified

Safety incidents by business unit

Percentage of stock unaccounted for
after stocktake

Level of client surveys

Percentage of clearance errors

Percentage of security incursions

Security incursions per employee

Percentage of safety equipment
checked per schedule

Number of safety accidents per 100
hours worked

Number of safety suggestions

GLOSSARY OF TERMS

Over the years, performance measurement theory has developed its own language. This is no different from accounting theory, business finance theory or organisational theory, each of which uses a highly technical set of terms. The following terms and definitions are used throughout this book, unless the context otherwise requires.

Audit A planned and documented activity performed to determine by investigation, examination or evaluation of objective evidence the adequacy of and compliance with established procedures, instructions, drawings and other applicable documents and the effectiveness of implementation.

Also, a systematic check to determine the quality of operation of a function or activity. Audits may be of two basic types: (1) *performance audits* in which quantitative data are independently obtained for comparison with routinely obtained data in a measurement system; and (2) *system audits* of a qualitative nature that consist of an on-site review of an organisation's quality system and physical facilities for sampling, calibration and measurement.

Balanced scorecard A method of measuring and managing business performance giving a balanced view of financial and operational perspectives to accelerate the management process.

Benchmark A standard or point of reference for measurement. By providing ranges or averages, benchmarks enable an organisation to compare performance in certain key areas with other organisations.

Benchmarking A method of measuring a process, system or outcome within an organisation against those of a recognised leader. The purpose of benchmarking is to provide a target for improved performance. Also, the process of comparing and measuring an organisation's own performance on a particular process against the performance of organisations judged to be the best in a comparable industry.

Benchmarking partner An entity whose processes you compare with your own processes.

Bottom up Starting with input from the people who actually do the work and consolidating that input through successively higher levels of management.

Business process re-engineering The fundamental rethinking and radical redesign of business processes to bring about dramatic improvements in critical, contemporary measures of performance, such as cost, quality, service and speed.[63]

This approach emphasises the breakthrough performance improvements that an organisation can realise by a process of *process redesign*.

Capital charge A dollar amount determined by multiplying the cost of capital by the capital employed.

Capital employed All the money tied up in property, equipment, computers and other things expected to be productive for some years after they have been purchased, and working capital such as trade debtors and inventories, less trade creditors and accrued expenses.

Characteristics Any property or attribute of an item, process or service that is distinct, describable and measurable.

Competitive advantage Consists of either a lower cost position than the organisation's competitors or the ability to achieve higher prices as a result of some perceived uniqueness in the market. The link between competitive advantage and success is borne out time after time by experience. Organisations that do not have a tangible competitive advantage rarely prosper for very long. They may grow in size while the market is growing or when competition is not intense. They are extremely unlikely to perform in the long term, however. Sooner or later the market's growth slows, and competitive pressures mount. When this happens, such firms' performance deteriorates rapidly. This link between profitability and competitive advantage is the very cornerstone of strategy.[64]

Continuous improvement The continuous

improvement of a process based on constant measurement and analysis of results produced by the process and use of that analysis to modify the process.

Also, where performance gains achieved are maintained and early identification of deteriorating performance levels is accomplished.

Corrective action Measures taken to rectify conditions adverse to quality and, where necessary, to preclude repetition.

Cost of capital The percentage return that the shareholders and lenders of the organisation would expect to receive each year if, instead of investing their capital in the organisation, they invested in an equally sound organisation. Put another way, it is the opportunity cost of capital.

Criteria The rules or tests against which the quality of performance can be measured. They are most effective when expressed quantitatively. Fundamental criteria can be enshrined in policies and objectives, as well as codes, standards, regulations, and recognised professional practices that employees are required to observe.

Data Factual information, regardless of media and format, used as a basis for reasoning, discussion or calculation.

Detailed in-process measure A measure to understand, optimise or control the process. They are used in the daily management of that process. Detailed in-process measures are measures of effectiveness and are lead indicators of sub-process performance. 'Time to take an order' is an example of a detailed in-process measure.

ETA The estimated time to arrival.

Effectiveness The ability to accomplish a desired result or to fulfill a purpose or intent.

Efficiency The quality or degree of effective operations as measured against cost, resources and time.

Goal A statement of the desired result to be achieved within a specified time. Goals are clear targets for specific action. More detailed than objectives, goals have shorter time frames. A goal is achievable, measurable, and sets the direction for strategies. A single objective may be subdivided into multiple goals.

Guideline A suggested practice that is not mandatory in programs intended to comply with a standard. The word 'should' or 'may' denotes a guideline; the word 'shall' or 'must' denotes a requirement.

Implementation The process that translates the *strategies* into actions in order to accomplish objectives.

Innovative lead time The time between the inception of an innovation and its introduction as a successful product or service into the marketplace.

Item An all-inclusive term used in place of the following; appurtenance, sample, assembly, component, equipment, material, module, part, structure, subassembly, subsystem, unit, documented concepts or data.

Lag indicator A measure which quantifies some characteristic after an event.

Lead indicator A measure with proven predictive ability with respect to some outcome.

Lessons learned A summary, intended for the beneficial use of the receiver, of conditions detected at any facility that may include techniques and actions employed to correct the condition.

A 'good work practice' or innovative approach that is captured and shared to promote repeat application. A lesson learned may also be an adverse work practice or experience that is captured and shared to avoid recurrence.

Line manager Includes all managers in the chain of command from the first-line supervisors to the top manager.

Liquidity crisis Insufficient cash to pay your financial obligations as they become due.

Management All individuals directly responsible and accountable for planning, implementing and assessing work activities.

Mean The arithmetic average of a set of numbers.

Measurement The quantitative parameter used to ascertain the degree of performance.

Metric Used synonymously with measurement.

Metrics Standards of measurement (such as length, area, frequency, mass and so on).

Mission statement See *Vision statement.*

Objective The result that an organisation aims to accomplish. Also, a statement of attainment/achievement, which is proposed to be accomplished or attained with an implication of sustained effort and energy. Objectives are the general ends toward which an organisation directs its efforts. Objectives address the primary issues confronting an organisation within broad groupings of interrelated concerns (client, financials, internal processes, and learning and growth). These objectives are founded on the corporate vision. Objectives are also known as critical success factors.

Occurrence An unusual or unplanned event having problematic significance such that it adversely affects or potentially affects the performance, reliability or safety of a facility.

Operational definition A consistent, reproducible, unambiguous standard that is understood by all relevant people. (For example, in the case of process measures, it will say precisely what is to be measured and how to measure it.)

Overview in-process measure A measure of process performance, frequently aggregated from detailed in-process measures. They are lead indicators of process performance (total or sub-process) and are used by management to monitor process performance, benchmark current best known practice and to focus process improvement. They are required for each and every client requirement. 'Total repair time' is an example of an overview in-process measure.

Performance indicators and indexes Dealing with these gets complicated because people can use them in very different ways, and there is no one standard to which you can appeal. Some use *indicator* and *measure* interchangeably, while others see *indicators* as subsets of *measures*. Others see *indicators* as sets of related measures. Still others prefer *indexes*, often thought of as sets of related measures (sometimes individually weighted) that track changes compared with a reference. For example, the Consumer Price Index measures inflation by combining the prices of selected goods and comparing the results over time. Other examples include an Index of Indicators (*Business Week*) that report various areas of the economy (production, construction etc.).

Performance measures Tools or indicators of an organisation's actions in achieving a given objective or goal. Performance measures can generally be divided into financial and non-financial measures. Non-financial measures are: client-oriented measures, internal business process measures and continuous improvement measures.

Process capability The limits of inherent variability within which a process operates are governed by the prevailing circumstances. The process capability measures the degree of predictability of process outcomes.

Process effectiveness measure Measures are used to assess, analyse, optimise and control the capability of the process to deliver outputs that satisfy client requirements.

Process stability A process that is in statistical control, and has an outcome that is random (yet predictable) within defined limits.

Profit After Tax (PAT) The earnings left over after deducting all the operating expenses, including depreciation and tax, but excluding interest.

Quality The degree to which a product or service meets client requirements and expectations.

Quality actions Actions that provide con-

fidence that quality is achieved.

Quality management The management of a process to maximise client satisfaction at the lowest cost.

Re-engineering A process of rethinking and redesigning internal business processes to achieve noticeable improvements in service delivery responsiveness to client needs and/or achieve significant reductions in cost.

Results measure A measure, from a client perspective, of the extent to which the process or product has met their requirement. These are lag indicators of process performance and therefore cannot be used as management tools in the daily control of processes. 'Client Satisfaction' is an example of a results measure.

Self-assessment A systematic evaluation of an organisation's performance, with the objectives of finding opportunities for improvement and exceptional practices; normally performed by the people involved in the activity, but may also be performed by others within the organisation with an arms-length relationship to the work processes.

Senior management The manager or managers responsible for mission accomplishment and overall operations.

Sensor A device that is able to sense the presence or absence of some phenomena and provide a reading of the level of that phenomena in a quantifiable form.

Site The area comprising the organisation's facilities.

Situation analysis The assessment of trends, strengths, weaknesses, opportunities and threats, giving a picture of the organisation's internal and external environment to determine the opportunities or obstacles to achieving organisational goals; performed in preparation for strategic planning efforts.

Stakeholder Any group or individual who is affected by or who can affect the future of an organisation—clients, employees, suppliers, owners, other agencies, government and critics.

Strategic decision A decision that externally re-positions an organisation in some way. That is, it changes the competitiveness of an organisation in its industry.

Strategic planning A process for helping an organisation envision what it hopes to accomplish in the future, identify and understand obstacles and opportunities that affect the organisation's ability to achieve that vision, and set forth the plan of activities and resource use that will best enable the achievement of the goals and objectives. Strategic planning is a long-term, future-oriented process of assessment, goal setting and decision making that maps an explicit path between the present and a vision of the future, relies on careful consideration of the business capabilities and competitive environment, and leads to priority-based resource allocation.

Strategy Strategies are methods to achieve goals and objectives. Formulated from goals and objectives, a strategy is the means of transforming inputs into outputs, and ultimately outcomes, with the best use of the available resources. A strategy reflects budgetary and other resources. The word 'strategy' is derived from the Greek military term *strategos,* literally meaning 'the general's art' Hofer and Schendel have defined the roles of corporate vision, division, and functional strategies, along with their interrelationships:[65]

• *Corporate strategy*: a plan that specifies two areas of overall interest to a company: (1) the definition of the business of the organisation; and (2) the acquisition and allocation of corporate resources to support each of these businesses.

• *Business strategy*: a plan specifying the scope of a given business and its link to the corporation's strategy. A business strategy specifies how a business unit will achieve and maintain its competitive advantage.

• *Functional strategy*: a plan created for marketing, manufacturing, research and development, finance, distribution, field services etc. Each functional strategy reinforces and supports the business strategy.

Christensen et al. have defined five characteristics of strategy:[66]

a Time horizon: an extended period of time.

b Impact: the result of pursuing a given strategy.

c Concentration of effort: a focus on a narrow range of activities.

d Pattern of decisions: decisions made over time which must be supportive of and consistent with one another.

e Pervasiveness: the extent to which all layers and functional units of an organisation reinforce and support the strategy.

System An interconnected set of processes, and a process is a set of activities that produce products or services (results). Products and services are treated alike; that is, the output of a process might be a product (like computer boards) or a service (like training).

Task A well-defined unit of work having an identifiable beginning and end that is a measurable component of the duties and responsibilities of a specific job.

Top down To start with the highest level of management in an organisation and propagating through successively lower levels of the organisation.

Total Quality Management (TQM) A management philosophy that involves everyone in an organisation in controlling and continuously improving how work is done in order to meet client expectations of quality.

Also, the management practice of continuous improvement in quality that relies on active participation of both management and employees using analytical tools and teamwork.

Unit of measure A defined amount of some quality feature that permits evaluation of that feature in numbers.

Validation A determination that an improvement action is functioning as designed and has eliminated the specific issue for which it was designed.

Also, to determine or test the truth or accuracy by comparison or reference.

Verification A determination that an improvement action has been implemented as designed.

Also, the process of evaluating hardware, software, data or information to ensure compliance with stated requirements. The act of reviewing, inspecting, testing, checking, auditing or otherwise determining and documenting whether items, processes, services or documents conform to specified requirements.

Vision statement A vision statement is an inspiring picture of an organisation's preferred future. A vision is not bound by time. It represents global and continuing purposes, and serves as a foundation for a system of strategic planning. A vision depicts an ideal future for an organisation. A vision must be leader initiated, shared and supported, as comprehensive as detailed, and inspiring.

John Browne, head of British Petroleum, prefers to think of vision in terms of the *purpose* of the organisation. By purpose he means who the organisation is and what makes it distinctive. It is what the organisation as a whole exists to achieve. Distinctive means that which gives the company a competitive edge or which serves as a competitive barrier.[67]

Work A process of performing a defined task or activity; for example, research and development, operations, maintenance and repair, administration, software development and use.

Also, the process of performing a defined task or activity; for example, research and development, operations, maintenance and repair, administration, software development and use, inspection, safeguards and security, data collection, and analysis.

REFERENCES

C. Y. BALDWIN, K. B. CLARK, 'Capabilities and Capital Investment: New Perspectives on Captial Budgeting' (1992) 5 *Journal of Applied Corporate Finance* 2, Summer, pp. 67–82.

C.I. BARNARD, *The Functions of the Executive*, Harvard University Press, Cambridge, MA., 1962.

M. BEER, R. RUH, J. A. DAWSON, M. J. KAVANAGH, 'A Performance Management System: Research, Design, Introduction and Evaluation' (1978), 31 *Personnel Psychology* 505.

S. BUNGAY, M. GOOLD, 'Creating a Strategic Control System' (1991), 24 *Long Range Planning* 3, 32.

R. D. BUZZELL, B. T. GALE, *The PIMS Principles: Linking Strategy to Performance,* Macmillan, New York, 1987.

R. C. CAMP, *Benchmarking—The Search for Industry Best Practices that Lead to Superior Performance,* ASQS Quality Press, Milwaukee, Wisconsin, 1989.

B. S. CHAKRAVARTHY, 'Measuring Strategic Performance' (1988), 7 *Strategic Management Journal* 110.

W. B. CHEW, 'No-nonsense Guide to Measuring Productivity' (1988), 66 *Harvard Business Review* 110.

R. COOPER, 'The Rise of Activity-Based Cost Systems: Part I—What is an Activity-Based Cost System?' (1988) *Journal of Cost Management,* Summer, p. 45.

C. S. CRAIG, S. P. DOUGLAS, 'Strategic Factors Associated with Market and Financial Performance' (1982) 22 *Quarterly Review of Economics and Business*, pp. 2, 101.

C. E. CRAIG, C. R. HARRIS, 'Total Productivity Measurement at the Firm Level' (1973), 14 *Sloan Management Review*, pp. 3, 13.

J. R. DIXON, A. J. NANNI, T. E. VOLLMANN, *The New Performance Challenge—Measuring Operations for World-Class Competition*, Dow Jones-Irwin, Homewood, Illinois, 1990.

R. G. ECCLES, 'The Performance Measurement Manifesto' (1991), *Harvard Business Review*, January–February, p. 131.

R. G. ECCLES, P. J. PYBURN, 'Creating a Comprehensive System to Measure Performance', (1992) *Management Accounting (US)*, October, p. 41.

L. FITZGERALD, R. JOHNSTON, T. J. BRIGNALL, R. SILVESTRO, C. VOSS, *Performance Measurement in Service Businesses*, CIMA, London, 1991.

L. FITZGERALD, P. MOON, *Performance Measurement in Service Industries: Making it Work*, The Chartered Institute of Management Accountants, London, 1996.

E. M. GOLDRATT, J. COX, *The Goal: Beating the Competition*, Creative Output Books, Hounslow, 1986.

V. GOVINDARAJAN, A. K. GUPTA, 'Linking Control Systems to Business Unit Strategy: Impact on Performance' (1985), 10 *Accounting, Organisations and Society*, pp. 1, 51.

R. W. HALL, H. T. JOHNSON, P. B. B. TURNEY, *Measuring Up—Charting Pathways to Excellence*, Irwin, Homewood, IL, 1991.

J. H. HOROVITZ, 'Strategic Control: A New Task for Top Management' (1979), 12 *Long Range Planning*, pp. 12, 2.

H. T. JOHNSON, R. S. KAPLAN, *Relevance Lost—The Rise and Fall of Management Accounting*, Harvard Business School Press, Boston, MA, 1987.

T. O. JONES, W. E. SASSER, 'Why Satisfied Customers Defect' (1995), 73 *Harvard Business Review* 6.

R. S. KAPLAN, 'Devising a Balanced Scorecard Matched to Business Strategy' (1994), September–October, *Planning Review* p. 15.

R. S. KAPLAN, D. P. NORTON, 'The Balanced Scorecard—Measures that Drive Performance' (1992), *Harvard Business Review*, January–February, p. 71.

R. S. KAPLAN, D. P. NORTON, 'Putting the Balanced Scorecard to Work' (1993), *Harvard Business Review*, September–October, p. 134.

R. S. KAPLAN, D. P. NORTON, 'Using the Balanced Scorecard as a Strategic Management System' (1996), *Harvard Business Review*, January–February, p. 75.

R. S. KAPLAN, D. P. NORTON, *The Balanced Scorecard—Translating Strategy into Action*, Harvard Business School Press, Boston, MA, 1996.

M. E. PORTER, 'What is Strategy?' (1996), *Harvard Business Review*, November–December, p. 78.

A. RAPPAPORT, *Creating Shareholder Value*, The Free Press, New York, NY, 1986.

R. J. SCHONBERGER, *Building a Chain of Customers*, Guild Publishing, London, 1990.

R. SIMONS, *Levers of Control: How Managers Use Control Systems to Drive Strategic Renewal*, Harvard Business School Press, 1995.

M. S. SLATER, 'Tailor Incentive Compensation to Strategy' (1973), *Harvard Business Review*, March–April, p. 94.

ENDNOTES

1   T. E. Vollman, 'Foreword', *Managing Human Resources: Integrating People and Business Strategy*, Business One Irwin, Homewood, 1992.

2   My last count was over four years ago. I cannot imagine how many new definitions there are today.

3   It is equally true to say that a properly designed performance measurement system is a crucial step for shop-floor workers to understand the centrality of the issue of shareholder wealth creation.

4   I gratefully acknowledge James McGrath's article, in which he expressed the passage in the most succinct and elegant manner and which I have reproduced here, *The Australian Financial Review*, 'Adding Value to the Boardroom', 10 June 1997, p. 19.

5   James McGrath, *The Australian Financial Review*, 'Adding Value to the Boardroom', 10 June 1997, p. 19.

6   R. J. Schonberger, *World Class Manufacturing: The Lesson of Simplicity Applied*, The Free Press, New York, 1986.

7   A. Lochamy and J. F. Fox, *Reengineering Performance Measurement*, Irwin, New York, 1994.

8   ICAA, 'What Makes a World-Class Organisation?' (1997), 7 *Charter* 40.

9   K. Feldmann, 'The Role of Strategy in Planning or Change' (1996), 9 *Management* 14.

10 K. Feldmann, 'The Role of Strategy in Planning or Change' (1996), 9 *Management* 14.

11 F. E. Jandt, *Win–Win Negotiating—Turning Conflict into Agreement*, John Wiley & Sons, New York, 1985, p. 112.

12 K. Feldmann, 'The Role of Strategy in Planning or Change' (1996), 9 *Management* 14.

13 R. H. Schaffer, *The Breakthrough Strategy*, Harper Business, USA, 1988.

14 A. M. Moodie, 'Leaders found key contrasts in corporate culture', The Australian Financial Review, http://www.afr.com.au/content/981113/surveysurvey3.html.

15 G. Haines, 'Don't Tinker—Transform!' (1996), 9 *Management* 11.

16 W. Fonvielle, *Client-Driven Measurement*, The Forum Corporation.

17 'Scoring the Scorecard', (1977), 3 *CFO* 43.

18 Business Intelligence, http://www.business-intelligence.co.uk.

19 J. Hyatt, 'Candela Laser Lays Off 30, Strategy Ills Blamed', *The Boston Globe*, May 1, 1993, p. 8.

20 R. S. Kaplan, D. P. Norton, 'The Balanced Scorecard—Measures that Drive Performance' (1992), *Harvard Business Review*, January–Febuary, p. 71; R. S. Kaplan, D. P. Norton, 'Putting the Balanced Scorecard to Work' (1993), *Harvard Business Review*, September–October, p. 134; R. S. Kaplan, D. P. Norton, 'Using the Balanced Scorecard as a Strategic Management System' (1996), *Harvard Business Review*, January–Febuary, p. 75.

21 Artificial Intelligence Applications Institute, 1996.

22 Artificial Intelligence Applications Institute, 1996.

23   (1996) 1 *Across the Board.*

24   Statement by R. S. Kaplan. Rennaisance website. July 1997. www.rens.com

25   N. Shoebridge, 'The Salary Game gets Churned up' (1997), *Business Book Weekly*, July 7, p. 36.

26   N. Shoebridge, 'The Salary Game gets Churned up' (1997), *Business Book Weekly*, July 7, p. 36.

27   L. Crosby, 'Measurements Exploding the Myths of Client Satisfaction Measurement', CSM Worldwide, Inc.

28   F. Reichheld, 'Learning from Customer Defections' (1996) *Harvard Business Review* March–April, p. 56.

29   L. Crosby, 'Measurements Exploding the Myths of Client Satisfaction Measurement', CSM Worldwide, Inc.

30   J. C. Anderson and J. Narns, 'Business Marketing: Understand what Customers Value' (1998), *Harvard Business Review* November–December, p. 53.

31   J. C. Unsunier, *International Marketing*, Business Book Summaries, p. 4.

32   M. O'Hare, *Innovate! How to Gain and Sustain Competitive Advantage,* Basil Blackwell, Oxford, 1998, p. 99.

33   J. Nelson, *Developing Effective External Client Satisfaction Surveys*, Reark Research P/L, 1994.

34   P. Drucker, 'Managing For The Future', *Business Book Summaries*, p. 7.

35   B. H. Maskell, *Making the Numbers Count—The Accountant as Change Agent On the World Class Team,* Productivity Press: Oregon, 1996, p. 147.

36   A. Lochamy, and J. F. Fox, *Reengineering Performance Measurement*, Irwin, New York, 1994.

37   www.ssb.rochester.edu/businessjournals/html/manage.html, 20/7/98.

38   Statement by R. S. Kaplan. Rennaisance website. July 1997. www.rens.com

39   A. Lochamy and J. F. Fox, *Reengineering Performance Measurement*, Irwin, New York, 1994.

40   A. Lochamy and J. F. Fox, *Reengineering Performance Measurement*, Irwin, New York, 1994.

41   E. M. Goldratt and R. Fox, *The Race*, North River Press, New York, 1986.

42   A. Lochamy and J. F. Fox, *Reengineering Performance Measurement*, Irwin, New York, 1994.

43   T. Nolan et al, *Plan or Die!*, Business Book Summaries, p. 4.

44   E. Hui, Business Intelligence, 1996, http://www.business-intelligence.co.uk.

45   T. Shaw, *How NRMA Achieves its Business Objectives by Satisfying The Client's Needs*, IIR Conferences, 1994.

46   'Scoring the Scorecard' (1997), 3 *CFO* 43.

47   R. S. Kaplan, D. P. Norton, 'The Balanced Scorecard—Measures that Drive Performance' (1992), *Harvard Business Review*, January–Feubary, p. 71; R. S. Kaplan, D. P. Norton, 'Putting the Balanced Scorecard to Work' (1993), *Harvard Business Review*, September–October, p. 134; R. S. Kaplan, D. P. Norton, 'Using the Balanced Scorecard as a Strategic Management System' (1996), *Harvard Business Review*, January–Feubary, p. 75.

48   T. J. Peters and R. H. Waterman, *In Search of Excellence: Lessons from America's Best-Run Companies* New York, Harper and Row, 1982.

49   T. J. Peters and R. H. Waterman, *In Search of Excellence: Lessons from America's Best-Run Companies* New York, Harper and Row, 1982, p. 311.

50   'Who's Excellent Now?', *Business Week*, 5 November 1984, p. 76.

51   N. Augustine, 'Reshaping an Industry: Lockheed Martin's Survival Story', *Harvard Business Review*, May–June 1997, p. 93.

52 M. Lawson, 'Culture Clashes Main Blight on M&As', *Australian Financial Review*, 16 November 1998, http://www.afr.com.au/content/981116/invest/invest3.html.

53 'Scoring the Scorecard' (1997), 3 *CFO* 43.

54 'Scoring the Scorecard' (1997), 3 *CFO* 43.

55 T. J. Larkin, 'Reaching and Changing Frontline Employees,' *Harvard Business Review*, May–June 1996, p. 99.

56 See F. E. Jandt, '*Win–Win Negotiating—Turning Conflict into Agreement*', John Wiley & Sons, New York, 1985.

57 E. Jacques and S. D. Clement, *Executive Leadership—A Practical Guide to Managing Complexity*, Oxford, Developmental Management, 1994, p. 155.

58 F. E. Jandt, '*Win–Win Negotiating—Turning Conflict into Agreement*', John Wiley & Sons, New York, 1985, pp. 109–110.

59 The Innovation Network, http://www.innovnet.com.

60 Compare that definition with the previous definition of benchmarking contained in Webster's Dictionary: 'A surveyor's mark... of previously determined position... and used as a reference point... standard by which something can be measured or judged.' Perhaps the most widely accepted definition is the one coined by David T. Kerns, CEO of Xerox, who said: 'Benchmarking is the continuous process of measuring products, services, and practices against the toughest competitors or those recognised as industry leaders.'

61 M. O'Hare, *Innovate! How to Gain and Sustain Competitive Advantage*, Basil Blackwell, Oxford, 1988, p. 59.

62 The Innovation Network, http://www.innovnet.com.

63 Hammer and Champy, *Reengineeing the Corporation*, 1993

64 M. O'Hare, *Innovate! How to Gain and Sustain Competitive Advantage*, Basil Blackwell, Oxford, 1988, pp. 35–6.

65 C. R. Hofer and D. Schendel, *Strategy Formulation: Analytical Concepts*, West Publishing, St Paul, 1978.

66 C. R. Christensen, K. R. Andrews, J. L. Bowers, R. G. Hammermesh, and M. E. Porter, *Business Policy* 5th ed., Richard D. Irwin: Homewood, 1982.

67 S. E. Prokesch, 'Unleashing the Power of Learning: An Interview with British Petroleum's John Browne', *Harvard Business Review*, September–October 1997, p. 146.

INDEX